Wie ist das Verhältnis zwischen Göttern und Menschen in Goethes "Prometheus" und Goethes "Ganymed" gestaltet?

Pia Ahnefeld

Bibliografische Information der Deutschen Nationalbibliothek:

Die Deutsche Nationalbibliothek verzeichnet diese Publikation in der Deutschen Nationalbibliografie; detaillierte bibliografische Daten sind im Internet über http://dnb.d-nb.de abrufbar.

ISBN: 9783346577986
Dieses Buch ist auch als E-Book erhältlich.

© GRIN Publishing GmbH
Nymphenburger Straße 86
80636 München

Druck und Bindung: Books on Demand GmbH, Norderstedt Germany
Gedruckt auf säurefreiem Papier aus verantwortungsvollen Quellen

Das vorliegende Werk wurde sorgfältig erarbeitet. Dennoch übernehmen Autoren und Verlag für die Richtigkeit von Angaben, Hinweisen, Links und Ratschlägen sowie eventuelle Druckfehler keine Haftung.

Das Buch bei GRIN: https://www.grin.com/document/1168386

Universität Siegen

Philosophische Fakultät

Germanistisches Seminar

Seminar: Ode und Lied um 1800

Sommersemester 2019

Seminararbeit: Wie ist das Verhältnis zwischen Göttern und Menschen in Goethes ‚Prometheus' und Goethes ‚Ganymed' gestaltet?"

Pia Ahnefeld

Inhaltsverzeichnis

1. Einleitung.. 3
2. Die epochale Einordnung der Hymnen 4
3. Prometheus Interpretation... 4
3.1. Zusammenfassung der Hymne und unterschiedliche Deutungsansätze........... 4
3.2. „Bedecke deinen Himmel, Zeus, Mit Wolkendunst!" – Deutungsansatz............ 8
4. Ganymed Interpretation.. 9
4.1. Zusammenfassung der Hymne und unterschiedliche Deutungsansätze........... 9
4.2. „Alliebender Vater!" – Deutungsansatz 11
5. Vergleich der beiden Hymnen in Bezug auf ihr Verhältnis zwischen Göttern und Menschen 11
6. Schlussteil... 12
7. Literaturverzeichnis 14

1. Einleitung

Die vorliegende Arbeit beschäftigt sich mit den beiden Hymnen „Prometheus" und „Ganymed" von Johann Wolfang von Goethe, die beide von der Beziehung zwischen Menschen und Göttern handeln. Goethe prägte mit seinen Hymnen die Epoche des Sturms und Drangs. Er schrieb „Prometheus" zwischen 1773 und 1774[1] und „Ganymed" 1774.[2] Die beiden Werke waren zunächst nicht für die Veröffentlichung bestimmt und diese erfolgte somit erst 1789. [3]

Die erst so gegensätzlich scheinende Beziehung zwischen Göttern und Menschen verändert sich bei der genaueren Betrachtung. Denn Goethes ‚Ganymed' und ‚Prometheus' bauen aufeinander auf und stehen somit in einem „korrelative[n] Verhältnis" zueinander.[4]

Die ersten beiden Verse der ‚Prometheus'-Hymne „Bedecke deinen Himmel, Zeus, Mit Wolkendunst!" und auch die ‚Ganymed'-Hymne im letzten Vers „Alliebender Vater!" beziehen sich sehr offensichtlich auf dieses Verhältnis zwischen Göttern und Menschen.

Während die Worte von Prometheus auf ein verachtendes Verhältnis hindeuten, wirken Ganymeds Worte eher liebevoll. Diese beiden unterschiedlichen Standpunkte lassen eine neue Weltanschauung Goethes und auch die scheinbare Religionskritik erahnen.

Die vorliegende Arbeit untersucht diese beiden Standpunkte Goethes und vergleicht unterschiedliche Forschungsansätze miteinander, geht auf Unterschiede und Gemeinsamkeiten ein und stellt anschließend einen Zusammenhang zwischen den beiden Hymnen dar. Im Anschluss an die Forschungsergebnisse erfolgt eine eigene Deutung und abschließend eine Einordnung in Bezug auf die Epoche des Sturms und Drangs und inwiefern diese Goethes Selbstverständnis verändert hat.

---

[1] Vgl.: Matthias Luserke-Jacqui: Goethes ‚Prometheus'-Ode: Text und Kontext. München. S.49.
[2] Vgl.: Hans-Georg Kemper: Herders Konzeption einer Mythopoesie und Goethes Ganymed. 1997. S.63.
[3] Vgl.: Joachim Heimerl: Systole und Diastole. 2001. S.78.
[4] Zitiert nach: Joachim Heimerl: Systole und Diastole. 2001. S.78.

2. Die epochale Einordnung der Hymnen

Die Epoche des Sturms und Drangs ist vor allem für das Gefühl, die Impulsivität und die freie Entfaltung bekannt. Diese Elemente werden sowohl in Prometheus als auch in Ganymed integriert. Ein weiteres relevantes Stichwort der Epoche ist die Gesellschaftskritik, welche ebenfalls in beiden Hymnen ausformuliert wird.

Diese Einordnung ist relevant, da diese Gedanken Goethes auf ein neues Selbstverständnis seinerseits schließen lassen und somit der persönliche Bezug zu den beiden Werken in den Fokus rückt.

Matthias Luserke-Jacqui betrachtet die Prometheus-Hymne als „Programm der Absage an ein tradiertes Literaturverständnis […], gleichsam als eine metaphorische Poetik des Sturm und Drang."[5] Es gebe kaum einen „respektloseren und damit provokanteren Text als Goethes Prometheus-Ode, der die Themen der individuellen Selbstbestimmung, des Selbsthelfertums, der Rebellion gegen die väterliche Ordnung und die poetologische Selbstrechtfertigung auf solch unterschiedlichen Sinn- und Verweisungsebenen formuliert."[6] Diese Behauptungen werden im Folgenden genauer untersucht.

3. Prometheus Interpretation

3.1. Zusammenfassung der Hymne und unterschiedliche Deutungsansätze

„Das Gedicht lebt von Mehrdeutigkeit". [7] Mit diesen Worten beschreibt Matthias Luserke-Jacqui die Komplexität der Interpretationsmöglichkeiten der „Prometheus"-Hymne. Mit den Possessivpronomen in V. 6 „meine Erde", V. 8 „meine Hütte" und V. 10 „meinen Herd" schaffe Prometheus seine eigene Welt unabhängig von den Göttern. In den verachtenden Versen der zweiten Strophe distanziere sich Prometheus erneut von den Göttern.[8] Laut Luserke-Jacqui gehe es bei Goethe „um Machtanspruch und Machtverteilung, ja

---

[5] Zitiert nach: Matthias Luserke-Jacqui: Goethes ‚Prometheus'-Ode: Text und Kontext. München. S.54.
[6] ebd.
[7] ebd., S.55.
[8] Vgl.: Matthias Luserke-Jacqui: Goethes ‚Prometheus'-Ode: Text und Kontext. München. S.50.

Gebietsverteilung: den Himmel dem Zeus, die Erde dem Prometheus".[9] Der regelmäßige Bezug auf seine Kindheit, soll seine Entwicklung hin zum Rebell demonstrieren, die den Ursprung in der Enttäuschung von Zeus habe.[10] Prometheus handele also nicht intuitiv, sondern aus Erfahrung.[11] Luserke-Jacqui sehe in der dritten Strophe einen deutlichen Bezug zu Korinther 13,11 und Matthäus 11,15, welche den Zusammenhang zu der vermuteten Religionskritik am Anfang darstellen soll. Die Begriffe „Klage" (V. 26) und „Herz" (V. 27) seien für ihn ebenfalls aus dem religiösen Begriffsinventar.[12] Zusammenfassend betrachtet er Prometheus als „Widerständler gegen herrschende Normen" und den Göttervater Zeus als „projizierte Vaterfigur oder als despotischer Landesfürst".[13]

Auch Johannes Windrich ist der Ansicht, dass Prometheus eine „haßerfüllte Rede gegen Zeus" sei.[14] Er denkt außerdem, dass der alte Glaube als eine naive Projektion von Kindern und Bettlern abgetan werde. Dies werde vor allem in Strophe zwei deutlich, wo Prometheus verachtende Worte an die Götter richte. Das Herz des Ichs sei nicht länger im Himmel, dennoch gebe es „Glut" (Vers 11), welche dafürstehe, dass das Feuer noch nicht erloschen sei. Diese Glut diene der Produktion der Geschöpfe, die er schaffe und sich damit selbst vervielfältige. Als Ersatz der Götter wird die Anwendung der eigenen Schöpferkraft in V. 52-54 genannt.[15] Der ehemalige Glaube an die Götter wird in Strophe drei (Vers 22 bis 28) betont, in dem Windrich das Bild des „Blicks oder des Glühens" verwendet.[16] Prometheus frühere Betrachtung des Olymps „war also eine des Auges bzw. der Helligkeit".[17]

Karl Maurer bezeichnet die Prometheus-Hymne als „dramatisches Rollengedicht" und stellt den „Mittler Prometheus" dem „Mittler Christus"

---

[9] ebd., S.50.
[10] ebd., S.51.
[11] Vgl. Matthias Luserke-Jacqui: Goethes ‚Prometheus'-Ode: Text und Kontext. München. S.51.
[12] Vgl. Matthias Luserke-Jacqui: Goethes ‚Prometheus'-Ode: Text und Kontext. München. S.51.
[13] Zitiert nach: Matthias Luserke-Jacqui: Goethes ‚Prometheus'-Ode: Text und Kontext. S.54.
[14] Zitiert nach: Johannes Windrich: Götter im Zwielicht. Zur Hymnendichtung des jungen Goethe. 2012. S.162.
[15] Vgl.: Johannes Windrich: Götter im Zwielicht, S.163.
[16] Zitiert nach: Johannes Windrich: Götter im Zwielicht. 2012. S.162.
[17] ebd., S.162f.

gegenüber.[18] Maurer knüpft damit an einen Ansatz von Karl Kerényi an: „Prometheus steht für die Menschheit ein, macht gemeinsame Sache mit ihr wie kein anderer Griechengott. Darin liegt die Ähnlichkeit mit der Beziehung Christi zur Menschheit. Doch Christus erleidet die menschliche Existenz als Mensch. […] Prometheus erscheint nie als Mensch."[19] Des Weiteren stellt Maurer den biografischen Bezug in der Hymne zu Goethes Lebenssituation her. In V. 43 „Hat nicht mich zum Manne geschmiedet" werde die Emanzipation von seinem Kinderglauben beschrieben und Goethe sei zu diesem Zeitpunkt ebenfalls selbst gerade „zum Manne geschmiedet" worden, da er zum Zeitpunkt der Verfassung des Gedichts erst 24 Jahre alt gewesen sei.[20] Zeus sei nicht allmächtig (V. 44 bis 46) und Prometheus beuge sich diesem Gott auch nicht.[21]

Christian Weber benennt das Thema der Ode als „Generalkritik der Einbildungskraft".[22] Für Weber symbolisiert die Glut die „Einbildungskraft und impliziert als solche die Möglichkeit, daß sich Menschen von den dominierenden mytho-theologischen Bildern durch das Schmieden von Gegenbildern befreien".[23] In der letzten Strophe beziehe sich die Hymne erneut auf die menschliche Einbildungskraft („Heilig glühend Herz?").[24] Die Substantive „Hütte" (V. 8), „Herd" (V. 10) und „Glut" (V. 11) seien „Produkte der Erde".[25] Durch diese Begriffe versuche er Zeus den „mündig werdenden Menschen" zu demonstrieren und, dass er feste auf der Erde stehe, auch wenn Zeus in das Weltgeschehen eingreifen möchte.[26] Weber geht ebenfalls auf die Kindheit von Prometheus und seinen ehemaligen Glauben ein, in der er an einen Gott geglaubt habe, was sich in V. 26ff. zeigt.[27] Die Substantive „Klage" (V. 26), „Bedrängten" und „erbarmen" (V. 28) lassen ebenfalls auf

---

[18] Zitiert nach: Karl Maurer: Prometheus – göttlicher Mittler oder Rebell?. Dodrecht. S. 18.
[19] Karl Kerényi, Prometheus, Die menschliche Existenz in griechischer Deutung, 1959, S.10, zitiert nach Karl Maurer: Prometheus – göttlicher Mittler oder Rebell?. Dodrecht. S. 22.
[20] Vgl.: Karl Maurer: Prometheus – göttlicher Mittler oder Rebell?. Dodrecht. S. 19.
[21] Vgl.: Karl Maurer: Prometheus – göttlicher Mittler oder Rebell?. Dodrecht. S. 19.
[22] Zitiert nach: Christian Weber: Goethes Prometheus: Kritik der poetischen Einbildungskraft. 2009. S.103.
[23] ebd., S.106.
[24] Vgl.: Christian Weber: Goethes Prometheus. 2009. S.113.
[25] ebd., S.107.
[26] ebd.
[27] Vgl.: Christian Weber: Goethes Prometheus. 2009. S.111.

einen christlichen Kontext schließen. Somit wird auch von Weber der theologische Bezug hergestellt.[28]

Auch Joachim Heimerl stellt einen christlichen Bezug her. Die Hymne sei wie bei Paulus in sieben Teile gegliedert. Christlich gehe es allerdings um die stufenweise Annäherung zu Gott. In Prometheus gehe es um stufenweise Abkehr von der Gottheit.[29] Deshalb bezeichnet er die Hymne auch als „Abgrenzung von [der] Gottheit".[30] „Meine Hütte" (V. 8) und „meinen Herd" (V. 10) bezeichne den realen Charakter der Welt.[31] „Hütte" (V. 8) und „Herd" (V. 10) würden dabei auch „für den Ersatz des gescheiterten Elternbildes und des vergeblichen Wunsches nach Trost und Geborgenheit […] und zugleich für eine fast therapeutische Bewältigung des kindlichen Desiderats nach Identifikationsfiguren" stehen.[32] In den Versen 16, 17 und 21 der dritten Strophe („Von Opfersteuern", „Und Gebetshauch" und „Hoffnungsvolle Toren") soll das übernatürlich Göttliche unterstrichen werden.[33] Durch den Wechsel der Anredeform von „Du" (V. 9, 12) zu „Euch" (V. 14) werde der Rückzug des Ichs in sich betont.[34] Prometheus sensible und emotionale Verfassung werde nicht beachtet und ignoriert (V. 22-28 und V. 38-41).[35] Heimerl greift ebenfalls erneut die Substantive „Klage" (V. 26) und „Herz" (V.27) auf und stellt einen Bezug zu Matthäus 11,15 her, denn es seien christliche Begriffe aus der Bibel.[36] In der vierten Strophe mit der Frage „Heilig glühend Herz?" stehe anstelle der Götter der „Wesenskern des autonomen Subjekts".[37] Die rhetorische Frage in der fünften Strophe (V. 43 bis 46) soll Prometheus Reifungsprozess symbolisieren und die väterliche Instanz erneut anklagen.[38] In der folgenden sechsten Strophe werden erneut die „antichristlichen Bezüge" aufgegriffen, um die Religion zu kritisieren.[39] Die

---

[28] Vgl.: Christian Weber: Goethes Prometheus. 2009. S.110.
[29] Vgl.: Joachim Heimerl: Systole und Diastole. 2001. S.87.
[30] Zitiert nach: Joachim Heimerl: Systole und Diastole. 2001. S.87.
[31] Vgl.: Joachim Heimerl: Systole und Diastole. 2001. S.86-87.
[32] Zitiert nach: Joachim Heimerl: Systole und Diastole. 2001. S.94.
[33] Vgl.: Joachim Heimerl: Systole und Diastole. 2001. S.90.
[34] Vgl.: Joachim Heimerl: Systole und Diastole. 2001. S.90.
[35] Vgl.: Joachim Heimerl: Systole und Diastole. 2001. S.93.
[36] Vgl.: Joachim Heimerl: Systole und Diastole. 2001. S.88.
[37] Zitiert nach: Joachim Heimerl: Systole und Diastole. 2001. S.84.
[38] Vgl.: Joachim Heimerl: Systole und Diastole. 2001. S.94.
[39] Zitiert nach: Joachim Heimerl: Systole und Diastole. 2001. S.88.

letzten Verse der Hymne gelten als „kindlicher Racheakt und Konsequenz eigener Subjektwerdung“.[40]

3.2. „Bedecke deinen Himmel, Zeus, Mit Wolkendunst!“ – Deutungsansatz

Der einleitende Satz („Bedecke deinen Himmel, Zeus, / Mit Wolkendunst!“ (V.1-2)) in Goethes Prometheus-Hymne lässt den Fortgang und den Inhalt des Gedichts vermuten. In den Versen der Hymne wird Zeus als der Göttervater betrachtet und gilt somit als höchster Gott im Olymp. Die Verse könnten somit auch als Kritik an der Religion gesehen werden, da Prometheus den Olymp mit dem Himmel gleichsetzt. Der Religionsbezug wird dadurch deutlich, dass Goethe hier auch explizit den Himmel und nicht den Olymp nennt, da er den christlichen Gott miteinschließt. Zeus soll den Himmel „bedecken“, weil Prometheus ihm dadurch signalisieren möchte, dass der Olymp, die Götter und die Religion nicht gebraucht werden.

Matthias Luserke-Jacqui deutet diesen Imperativ als Drohung gegen Zeus als Göttervater selbst. Die erste Strophe beschreibe, dass die Götter nicht die Erwartungen der Allmacht besäßen und Prometheus sich aus diesem Abhängigkeitsverhältnis lösen möchte.[41]

Auch Johannes Windrich sei dies „nicht nur eine Geste der Provokation, sondern zugleich ein Zeichen für die endgültige Aufgabe seiner früheren Haltung“.[42] Er bezeichnet die Hymne auch als „Anti-Hymne“.[43]

Laut Christian Weber versuche Prometheus „die Wiederkehr des ihm und seinem Werk feindlich gesinnten Zeus sofort wieder zu verscheuchen“.[44] Außerdem versuche Prometheus die „Umkehrung der politischen Mytho-Theologie“.[45] Er widerstrebe sich der Gewaltherrschaft von Zeus.[46]

Joachim Heimerl bezeichnet diese einleitenden Verse als „apodiktische Aufforderung an Zeus und mit ihm an jede herkömmliche transzendentale Gottesvorstellung, in einem Jenseits zu verschwinden, das als nichtiges

---

[40] ebd., S.95.
[41] Matthias Luserke-Jacqui: Goethes ‚Prometheus‘-Ode: Text und Kontext. München. S.50.
[42] Zitiert nach: Johannes Windrich: Götter im Zwielicht. 2012. S.163.
[43] ebd., S.162.
[44] Zitiert nach: Christian Weber: Goethes Prometheus: Kritik der poetischen Einbildungskraft. 2009. S.102.
[45] ebd., S.105.
[46] Vgl.: Christian Weber: Goethes Prometheus. 2009. S.106.

Abseits verstanden wird [...]".[47] Prometheus fordere damit die „absolute Scheidung menschlich-genialer (immanenter) und göttlicher (transzendentaler) Sphäre".[48] Er fordere den absoluten Rückzug Zeus von der Erde in seinen Himmel, diesen solle er „bedecken" (V. 1)[49] und er stelle den Himmel als „Jenseits" und die Erde als „Diesseits" gegenüber.[50] Die „Prometheus-irdische Sphäre" befreie sich „von den Autoritäts- und Besitzansprüchen der Gottheit".[51] Prometheus verweise die göttliche Allmacht wie ein Kind in die Schranken, in dem es in einen entfernten Raum verschwinde, der nur noch mit „Wolkendunst" (V. 2) bedeckt sei.[52]

4. Ganymed Interpretation

4.1. Zusammenfassung der Hymne und unterschiedliche Deutungsansätze

Johannes Windrich beschreibt die beginnenden Verse (V.1-3) der „Ganymed"-Hymne als „schwärmerische Anrede an die Frühlingsnatur".[53] Die Substantive „Morgenglanze" (V.1) und „Frühling" (V.3) würden auf eine Szene am Morgen und auf „erwachendes Licht" schließen lassen.[54] Ganymed sei im „Modus der Verehrung".[55] Laut Windrich nehme die „sehnsüchtige Umarmung zwischen Ich und Natur" im Laufe der Hymne zu.[56] Diese allmähliche Zuwendung an das Göttliche sei „von einer Eintrübung des Wetters begleitet".[57]

Joachim Heimerl bezeichnet Ganymed als „absolut harmonische[n] Konsens des prometheischen Genies" und schildert die Substantive „Liebeswonne" (V. 4), „Herz" (V. 5), „ewigen Wärme" (V.6) und „Heilig Gefühl," (V.7) in der ersten Strophe Ganymeds als Erfahrung durch Gott.[58] Das Herz des Ichs sei das

---

[47] Zitiert nach: Joachim Heimerl: Systole und Diastole. 2001. S.86.
[48] ebd.
[49] Vgl.: Joachim Heimerl: Systole und Diastole. 2001. S.86.
[50] Zitiert nach: Joachim Heimerl: Systole und Diastole. 2001. S.86.
[51] ebd., S.87.
[52] Vgl.: Joachim Heimerl: Systole und Diastole. 2001. S.87.
[53] Zitiert nach: Johannes Windrich: Götter im Zwielicht. Zur Hymnendichtung des jungen Goethe. 2012. S.159.
[54] ebd., S.161.
[55] ebd., S.165.
[56] ebd., S.159.
[57] ebd., S.160.
[58] Joachim Heimerl: Systole und Diastole. 2001. S.101.

„Medium der Erfahrbarkeit".[59] In V. 9 und 10 schildert er, dass das Ich die Unmöglichkeit von Vereinigung mit der Natur erkenne, aber gleichermaßen auf die Vereinigung mit der Gottheit hoffe.[60] Die Verse 20 und 21 gelten für ihn als ein Motiv der Bibel und könnten mit Christus gleichgesetzt werden, der ebenfalls in den Himmel auffahre. Das Ich strebe diesem Prozess selbst hingegen[61] und die Verse 20-21 gelten als Überleitung hierfür.[62] Diese Vereinigung mit der Gottheit finde ebenfalls in einem übernatürlichen Raum statt, was durch das Motiv der „Wolken" (V. 23 und 24) deutlich werde.[63]

Hans-Georg Kemper deutet die ganze erste Strophe der Ganymed-Hymne als Pulse zwischen Anspannung und Entspannung.[64] Die Personifizierung des Frühlings in V. 3 deute auf die Liebeskraft Gottes hin.[65] Auch die Bezeichnung „Unendliche Schöne" (V. 8) meine den Frühling[66] und deute auf den Verlust der Wahrnehmung des Auges hin. Der Verlust des Hörens werde in V. 18 deutlich.[67] Laut Kemper sei für Prometheus die gesamte „Erfahrung […] ganz sinnlich fundiert, die Emotionen äußern sich in körperlich-taktilen Aktionen und Reaktionen". Dies werde in V. 2 „anglühst", V. 5 „drängt", V. 9 „fassen", V. 12 „Lieg ich, schmachte", V. 14 „Drängen sich", V. 15 „kühlst", V. 22 „strebt's", V. 23 „schweben" und V. 25 „Neigen sich" deutlich.[68] Auch Kemper stellt einen religiösen Bezug her, indem er das „auffällige Miteinander von männlichen und weiblichen Attributen der Natur" als „Androgynie, die am Anfang der Schöpfung bestand und an deren Ende wiederhergestellt werden soll" nennt. Das „sprachliche Symbol 'Y'" sei auch „die Mitte des Names Ganymed".[69]

---

[59] Zitiert nach: Joachim Heimerl: Systole und Diastole. 2001. S.102.
[60] Vgl.: Joachim Heimerl: Systole und Diastole. 2001. S.106.
[61] Vgl.: Joachim Heimerl: Systole und Diastole. 2001. S.103.
[62] Vgl.: Joachim Heimerl: Systole und Diastole. 2001. S.106.
[63] Vgl.: Joachim Heimerl: Systole und Diastole. 2001. S.105.
[64] Vgl.: Hans-Georg Kemper: Herders Konzeption einer Mythopoesie und Goethes Ganymed. 1997. S.69.
[65] Vgl.: Hans-Georg Kemper: Herders Konzeption einer Mythopoesie und Goethes Ganymed. 1997. S.67.
[66] Vgl.: Hans-Georg Kemper: Herders Konzeption einer Mythopoesie und Goethes Ganymed. 1997. S.68.
[67] Vgl.: Hans-Georg Kemper: Herders Konzeption einer Mythopoesie und Goethes Ganymed. 1997. S.69.
[68] Zitiert nach: Hans-Georg Kemper: Herders Konzeption einer Mythopoesie und Goethes Ganymed. 1997. S.68.
[69] ebd.

4.2. „Alliebender Vater!" – Deutungsansatz

Ganymeds Hingabe zu Gott wird im Laufe des Gedichts durch die Motive des Frühlings, des Herzens, des Morgens und der Wolken deutlich. Diese Hingabe wird durch den letzten Vers „Alliebender Vater" (V.31) nochmals gesteigert. Es könnte hier sowohl ein väterliches, als auch ein göttliches Verhältnis gemeint sein.

Zu Beginn der letzten Strophe werde deutlich, dass sich die Wolken langsam senken würden und das Ich in Ihnen schwebe und währenddessen seine Gottheit rufe.[70] Laut Johannes Windrich unterstützen die Wolken das Ich bei der „Zusammenkunft mit der Gottheit".[71]

Joachim Heimerl deutet den Ruf in V. 29 „Umfangend umfangen!" als Vereinigung von Gott, Mensch und Natur und spricht von „universaler Harmonie".[72] Diese Harmonie habe ihren Höhepunkt in dem letzten Imperativ der Ganymed-Hymne „Alliebender Vater!".[73] Die Verschmelzung des Ichs mit der Natur gilt für ihn als „religiöses Ereignis".[74]

Hans-Georg Kemper betrachtet den „Alliebenden Vater" (V. 31) als finalen und zentralen Charakter für das Ich und das Gedicht.[75] Das Ich empfange in „Anglühen" (V. 2) und „kühlen" (V. 15) die Gottheit am Ende der Hymne. Die Aufwärtsbewegung verweise auf die Gottverbundenheit, der die Rückkehr in das Licht als erlösend wahrnehme.[76] Hierfür sprechen auch die Motive des „Schosse" (V. 27) und „Busen" (V.30), die für die Geborgenheit des Vaters stehen würden.[77]

5. Vergleich der beiden Hymnen in Bezug auf ihr Verhältnis zwischen Göttern und Menschen

Die beiden Texte stehen sich inhaltlich zwar gegenüber, weisen aber dennoch Zusammenhänge auf. Ganymed wird von Heimerl im Vergleich zu

---

[70] Vgl. Johannes Windrich: Götter im Zwielicht. 2012. S.161
[71] Zitiert nach: Johannes Windrich: Götter im Zwielicht. 2012. S.160.
[72] Zitiert nach: Joachim Heimerl: Systole und Diastole. 2001. S.109.
[73] Vgl.: Joachim Heimerl: Systole und Diastole. 2001. S.109.
[74] Zitiert nach: Joachim Heimerl: Systole und Diastole. 2001. S.104.
[75] Vgl.: Hans-Georg Kemper: Herders Konzeption einer Mythopoesie und Goethes Ganymed. 1997. S.74.
[76] Vgl.: Hans-Georg Kemper: Herders Konzeption einer Mythopoesie und Goethes Ganymed. 1997. S.69.
[77] Vgl.: Hans-Georg Kemper: Herders Konzeption einer Mythopoesie und Goethes Ganymed. 1997. S.68.

Prometheus „Verselbstung" als „Entselbstung" definiert.[78] Während sich Prometheus von der Gottheit abwende, suche Ganymed die Nähe zu Gott.[79] Beide Hymnen haben einen religiösen Bezug. Prometheus unterstreicht dies durch seine verachtenden Worte. Ganymed hingegen spricht liebevolle Worte zu Gott. In der Prometheus-Hymne wirkt es so, als ob ein Gewitter aufzieht, wobei hingegen Ganymed von „Morgenglanze" (V. 1) und „Frühling" (V. 3) spricht.

Im Vergleich zu Zeus sei „das Sehen bis zu einem gewissen grade wieder zugelassen [...]: Ganymed als sich öffnender, hymnischer Blick, [...] Prometheus als sich verschließende, auf das Selbst gerichtete Bewegung."[80]

6. Schlussteil

Um die vorliegende Fragestellung zu beantworten, kann man sagen, dass sich die Prometheus-Hymne durch verachtende und immer wieder aufgreifende Worte gegen die Götter stellt. Ganymed hingegen vergöttert ihre Gottheit.

Nachdem Goethe zuerst Prometheus und dann Ganymed verfasste, wird schnell deutlich, dass sich die Ganymed-Hymne auf die Prometheus-Hymne bezieht. Laut Joachim Heimerl kann dies „nur unter der Voraussetzung der zuvor in der Prometheus-Hymne thematisierten Abkehr vom alten, transzendentalen Gottesbild und der gleichzeitig damit vollzogenen Hinwendung zur diesseitigen Welt möglich werden, die im Pantheismus der Ganymed-Hymne schließlich ihre höchste Ausdruckskraft erreicht".[81] Denn laut Windrich wäre „Ohne Ganymed [...] nicht zu erkennen, inwiefern Prometheus einen Teil der Hymnenreihe bilden soll."[82] „Das Zusammenspiel der beiden Texte wird zudem immer wieder mit Hilfe der Goetheschen Begriffspaare von ‚Verselbstigung' und ‚Entselbstung' bzw. von Systole und Diastole beschrieben."[83] Laut Windrich stehen Prometheus und Ganymed in einem sich ergänzenden Verhältnis, denn in Prometheus „werde die Vorstellung eines extramundanen Gottes als naive Projektion entlarvt,

---

[78] Zitiert nach: Joachim Heimerl: Systole und Diastole. 2001. S.87.
[79] Vgl.: Joachim Heimerl: Systole und Diastole. 2001. S.87.
[80] Zitiert nach: Johannes Windrich: Götter im Zwielicht. 2012. S.163.
[81] Zitiert nach: Joachim Heimerl: Systole und Diastole. 2001. S.102.
[82] Zitiert nach: Johannes Windrich: Götter im Zwielicht. 2012. S.162.
[83] ebd.

Ganymed finde auf dem Boden der neuerrungenen Freiheit das Göttliche in der diesseitigen Natur."[84]

Kemper betrachtet Prometheus und Ganymed als „programmatische Höhepunkte der Selbstermächtigung des Subjekts im Sturm und Drang, indessen ist Ganymed über Prometheus hinaus bei aller Säkularisierung und nicht-christlichen Religiosität als Organ und Medium eines Augenblicks sich vollziehenden Vorgangs der Begegnung und Vereinigung mit der als göttlich erfahrenen Natur Ausdruck religiöser Empfindung und ‚Anbetung'".[85] Auch Heimerl schreibt, dass Goethe die Prometheus-Figur als „Symbol des Künstlers und insbesondere des dichterischen Genies" sehe.[86]

Die beiden Hymnen sind somit insofern bedeutend, dass sie auf ein neues Selbstverständnis Goethes durch die Epoche des Sturms und Drangs schließen lassen. Zu Beginn wurden die Beobachtungen Luserkes zitiert, dass Prometheus gegen die väterliche Ordnung rebelliere und Ganymed sich dieser zuwende, welche sich nun bestätigen lassen. Die beiden Hymnen sollen somit diese unterschiedlichen Standpunkte Goethes darstellen. Dies wird vor allem dadurch deutlich, als dass sie nicht für die Veröffentlichung bestimmt waren oder bzw. erst deutlich nach der Verfassung veröffentlicht wurden.

Durch „Hier sitz ich, forme Menschen / Nach meinem Bilde" (V. 52 bis 53) wird „nochmals latent eine autobiografische Referenz auf Goethe erkennbar, der in der Prometheus-Figur ein Abbild seines neuen künstlerischen Selbstverständnisses als dichterisches Genie kreiert das sich (am Schreibtisch) sitzend gleich Prometheus eine eigene (fiktive) Welt erschafft".[87] Der stärkere Bezug Goethes war zur Prometheus-Hymne, indem er gegen eine religiöse Ordnung, gegen staatliche Strukturen, gegen die Ständegesellschaft und gegen die bisherige dichterische Ordnung rebellieren wollte.

---

[84] ebd.
[85] Zitiert nach: Hans-Georg Kemper: Herders Konzeption einer Mythopoesie und Goethes Ganymed. 1997. S.76.
[86] Zitiert nach: Joachim Heimerl: Systole und Diastole. 2001. S.115.
[87] ebd., S.83.

7. Literaturverzeichnis

Beck, O. (2000). *Johann Wolfgang von Goethe Werke.* München: Deutscher Taschenbuch Verlag GmbH & CO. KG.

Heimerl, J. (2001). *Systole und Diastole - Studien zur Bedeutung des Prometheussymbols im Werk Goethes: Versuch einer Neubestimmung.* München: Judicium.

Kemper, H.-G. (1997). Herders Konzeption einer Mythopoesie und Goethes Ganymed. In: M. Bassler (Hrsg.), C. Brecht (Hrsg.), D. Niefanger (Hrsg.): *Von der Natur zur Kunst zurück: Neue Beiträge zur Goethe Forschung* (S.39-77). Tübingen: Niemeyer.

Luserke-Jaqui, M. (1996). Goethes ,Prometheus'-Ode: Text und Kontext. In G. Sauder (Hrsg.): *Goethe-Gedichte: zweiunddreißig Interpretationen* (S.47-57). München: Hanser Verlag.

Maurer, K. (1926). Prometheus – göttlicher Mittler oder Rebell?. In: *Neohelicon acta comparationis litterarum universarum* (S.18-22). Dodrecht: Springer Verlag.

Weber, C. (2009). Goethes Prometheus: Kritik der poetischen Einbildungskraft. In: *Goethe Yearbook* (S.101-133). North American Goethe Society.

Windrich, J. (2012). Götter im Zwielicht: Zur Hymnendichtung des jungen Goethe. *Poetica: Zeitschrift für Sprach- und Literaturwissenschaft,* 44, S.143.

Prabha Deo

A Systematic Approach To The Theory And Applications Of Probability

Theory and Applications of Probability

LAP LAMBERT Academic Publishing

Impressum / Imprint

Bibliografische Information der Deutschen Nationalbibliothek: Die Deutsche Nationalbibliothek verzeichnet diese Publikation in der Deutschen Nationalbibliografie; detaillierte bibliografische Daten sind im Internet über http://dnb.d-nb.de abrufbar.

Alle in diesem Buch genannten Marken und Produktnamen unterliegen warenzeichen-, marken- oder patentrechtlichem Schutz bzw. sind Warenzeichen oder eingetragene Warenzeichen der jeweiligen Inhaber. Die Wiedergabe von Marken, Produktnamen, Gebrauchsnamen, Handelsnamen, Warenbezeichnungen u.s.w. in diesem Werk berechtigt auch ohne besondere Kennzeichnung nicht zu der Annahme, dass solche Namen im Sinne der Warenzeichen- und Markenschutzgesetzgebung als frei zu betrachten wären und daher von jedermann benutzt werden dürften.

Bibliographic information published by the Deutsche Nationalbibliothek: The Deutsche Nationalbibliothek lists this publication in the Deutsche Nationalbibliografie; detailed bibliographic data are available in the Internet at http://dnb.d-nb.de.

Any brand names and product names mentioned in this book are subject to trademark, brand or patent protection and are trademarks or registered trademarks of their respective holders. The use of brand names, product names, common names, trade names, product descriptions etc. even without a particular marking in this work is in no way to be construed to mean that such names may be regarded as unrestricted in respect of trademark and brand protection legislation and could thus be used by anyone.

Coverbild / Cover image: www.ingimage.com

Verlag / Publisher:
LAP LAMBERT Academic Publishing
ist ein Imprint der / is a trademark of
OmniScriptum GmbH & Co. KG
Heinrich-Böcking-Str. 6-8, 66121 Saarbrücken, Deutschland / Germany
Email: info@lap-publishing.com

Herstellung: siehe letzte Seite /
Printed at: see last page
ISBN: 978-3-659-74152-4

A Systematic Approach
To The Theory And Applications of Probability

CONTENTS

Chapter 1	Introduction	3
Chapter 2	Basic Terms	4
Chapter 3	Fundamentals of Set Theory	8
Chapter 4	Events and their Probabilities	12
Chapter 5	Combinatorial Mathematics	19
Chapter 6	Probability Distribution	26
Chapter 7	Examples	36
Chapter 8	Applications of Probability Theory	54
	Bibiography	62

Chapter 1

INTRODUCTION

The Theory of Probability is one of the interesting topics in Statistics and Mathematics. The 'Probability' is the mathematical measure of a chance of occurrence of an uncertain event. In day-to-day life, man is always interested in predictions regarding future events, particularly uncertain ones like weather, lottery results, examination results and so on. The origin of the theory of probability is in the game of chance. However, the topic is so developed that it finds applications in Economics, Commerce, Industry and all branches of Engineering, Technology and Science.

Various terms are used in the theory of probability. One has to modify or supplement the dictionary meanings of these terms. The Chapter 'Basic Terms' is included to clearly describe these terms.

To understand and use the theory of probability, back up knowledge is a pre-requisite. Two chapters, one on Set Theory and other on Permutations & Combinations are included. In the chapter 'Events and their Probabilities' events are classified and methods to determine the probability of their occurrence is covered. The conditional and inverse probabilities are useful in case of complex events.

In the chapter 'Probability Distribution', a special term 'Random Variable' is introduced and the probability distributions of discrete and continuous variables are discussed. The most popular term in frequency and probability distribution is the 'normal curve'. This is mainly a topic from Statistics. Instead of detailed discussion, only those points related to the Theory of Probability are included. For detailed study of statistical aspects, one can refer to books listed in 'Bibliography' section. In chapter 7, various numerical examples are worked out. The aim of writing this book is to arrange the material available in various books in such a way as to establish a link between various aspects of the theory. On reading and understanding the theories given in this book, it is expected that a reader should be able to solve independently the majority of the problems given in the seventh chapter.

Study of any theory is incomplete without the study of its applications. Chapter 8 is devoted to applications. The author has taken pains to study of articles made available to her by "Google search" of this topic. School and college level students may or may not find this chapter useful. However, it is hoped that a person from any discipline who wishes to apply the probability to a specific problem of his interest shall find this chapter useful.

Any comments, any suggestions are welcome as that is a proof of the book's utility.

Chapter 2

BASIC TERMS

1)   Experiment

Experiment is defined as an activity, operation or action, which can produce some well-defined results or outcomes.

2)   Deterministic Experiments

These are experiments which, when repeated under identical conditions, produce almost same results. Here chance does not play any role in the outcome of experiment. In Science laboratories, deterministic experiments are carried out.

3)   Random Experiments

The examples of random experiments are *(a) Throwing a die, (b) Tossing a coin and (c) Picking out a card from a well-shuffled pack of cards.* In 'throwing a die' experiment, the possible results are 1, 2, 3, 4, 5, and 6. In a throw one is not sure that, which number will appear on the top? When a coin is tossed, you will get either 'Head' or 'Tail'. In 'Random experiment' when the experiment is repeated under identical conditions, the result may vary irregularly from one repetition or trial to another.

4)   Set

It is a well-defined collection of distinct objects. For example, A set of first three odd numbers is {1,3,5}.

5)   Subset

Consider two sets A and B. If each element of set B is an element of set A, then set B is a subset of set A. For example, let set A = {1,2,3,4,5},set B = {2,4}. The set B is a subset of the set A.

6)   Sample Space & Sample Points

The set of all possible outcomes of a random experiment is called a 'Sample space'. It is denoted by 'S'. Elements of Sample space are called 'Sample points'. The sample space of the random experiment 'tossing a coin' is, S = {H, T}. The sample space of a random experiment 'Throwing a die' is S = {1, 2, 3, 4, 5, 6}. These two examples have discrete sample space. A sample space is continuous in case of some random experiments. For example, consider the random experiment of shooting a target and measuring distance by which it misses the target. The sample space is a set $S = \{x: x \hat{I} R\}$. *Where R is a set of real numbers.* The property of a continuous sample space is that it has uncountable infinite number of sample points.

7)   Event

Any subset of a sample space is an event. A simple event consists of only one sample point. A complex event is decomposable into a number of simple events. A simple event is also called as an Elementary event.

8)   Occurrence of an event

An event E is a subset of a sample space of a random experiment. If W is the outcome of a trial of a random experiment and W is a subset of E, then it is said that the event E has occurred. If W is not a subset of E, then it is said that the event has not occurred. In a random experiment of 'Throwing a die', let an event 'E' be described as 'Getting an even number'. If the outcome, W, of a trial is 2, it is said that the event E has occurred.

9)   Favorable and Unfavorable Outcomes

When an outcome of a trial of a random experiment is a subset of event E, then it is said that it is a favourable outcome. If the outcome is not a subset of E then it is called as Unfavourable outcome. Consider the random experiment of 'Throwing a die'. Let the event E be 'Getting an even number'. The set E is $\{2, 4, 6\}$. Let the outcome of a trial be 4. Since $\{4\}$ is a subset of E, the outcome 4 is a favourable outcome. Let the outcome of another trial i.e. 'throw of a die' be 3. Since $\{3\}$ is not a subset of E, it is an unfavourable outcome.

10) Probability

It is a measure of uncertainty of events in a random experiment. It is a function of outcomes of a random experiment. The range of this function is a closed interval [0-1].Consider a simple random experiment 'Tossing a coin'. There are two equally likely outcomes. In hundred tosses, one expects to get 'head' fifty times, and get 'tail' fifty times. It is assumed that the coin is good or unbiased. Consider an event E 'Getting head'. Its probability is ½. Consider an event F 'Getting tail'. Its probability is also half. In case of complex events, the determination of probability is a complex process.

11) Mathematical or Apriori Probability

It is termed as apriori because it is determined prior to the occurrence of an event A. All possible discrete outcomes of a random experiment are listed as Sample space S. Let n(S) be the number of sample points. An event A is a subset of S including all sample points favourable to an event 'A'. Let n (A) be the number of sample points favourable to the event A.

The mathematical probability P (A) is defined as

$$P(A) = \frac{n(A)}{n(S)}$$

i.e. $P(A) = \dfrac{\textit{No. of favorable outcomes of event A}}{\textit{Total number of sample points of the random experiment}}$

Let us consider a random experiment of 'throwing a die'. Consider an event 'Getting an even number'. Let us denote this event by A. Sample space S of this experiment is {1, 2, 3, 4, 5, 6} and the event A is {2, 4, 6}. In case of random throw of an unbiased die, all possible outcomes are equally likely.

Therefore $P(A) = \dfrac{n(A)}{n(S)} = \dfrac{3}{6} = \dfrac{1}{2}$.

Thus the probability of the event A, getting an even number as an outcome of a

'random throw' is $\dfrac{1}{2} = 0.5$

12) Statistical Probability (posteriori)

Statistical probability is estimated by trial and observation. An experiment is repeated under essentially the same conditions. If an event A has occurred 'r' times in a series of 'n' independent trials then the statistical probability is given as,

$$P(A) = \frac{r}{n}$$

The probability obtained is the approximate value; 'n' should be sufficiently large to get good estimate. The definition of statistical probability is,

$$P(A) = \lim_{n \to \infty} \left(\frac{r}{n} \right)$$

In case of random experiments, if it is not possible to determine the number of all possible outcomes n(S), then mathematical probability cannot be found out. In such cases, statistical probability is found out by observing already available data or by repeating the experiment several times and generating the required data.

Let us consider one example. From mortality tables compiled in past years, it is found that out of 1,00,000 new born males, about 92,300 of them are alive at the age of 20. Estimate the probability that a newborn male will live to be 20 years old. The event A in this case is, 'a new born male will live to be 20years old.' From the given data r = 92,300 and n = 1, 00,000. Therefore estimated value of probability

$$P(A) = \frac{92,300}{1,00,000} = 0.923$$

13) Random Variable 'X'

A random variable is a real valued function X defined over the sample space of a random experiment. Consider a random experiment of 'throwing a fair die'. Let us consider an event E as 'Getting an even number'. Now let us denote by X the count of even numbers one gets in a single throw. The sample space S = {1, 2, 3, 4, 5, 6}. The event E is {2, 4, 6}. But X i.e. number of even numbers one gets in a throw, has two values X = 0 or X = 1. Consider another example. A random experiment is 'Tossing a coin thrice'. The event E is say 'Getting at least two tails'. The sample space S = {HHH, HHT, HTH, HTT, THH, THT, TTH, TTT}. The number of favourable outcomes is four. E = {HTT, THT, TTH, TTT} &

$P(E) = \frac{4}{8} = \frac{1}{2}$. Now let a random variable X be 'number of tails' one can get in tossing

a coin thrice. X can take one of the four values. 0 (no tail), 1, 2 or 3.

14) Probability Distribution Function

It is a relationship between a set of random variable X and the probability P(X). The Probability distribution function of a discrete random variable is represented as follows:

X	X_1	X_2	X_3	....	X_n
P(X)	$P(X_1)$	$P(X_2)$	$P(X_3)$	....	$P(X_n)$

Where all $P(Xi)$s are ≥ 0 and $\sum_{i=1}^{n} P(xi) = 1$ In the above mentioned example of

'Tossing a coin thrice' the probability distribution function is,

X	0	1	2	3
P(X)	1/8	3/8	3/8	1/8

X is the 'number of tails' & P(X) is the corresponding probability.

$$\sum_{i=1}^{4} P(xi) = \frac{1}{8} + \frac{3}{8} + \frac{3}{8} + \frac{1}{8} = 1$$

Chapter 3

FUNDAMENTALS OF SET THEORY

The basic operations in a Set theory are useful in determining the probability of compound events. Let us recapitulate the basic operations. Events are denoted by letters A, B, C... They are subsets of a sample space S.

1)   Set:

It is a well-defined collection of distinct objects. E.g. A set of first three odd numbers is $\{1, 3, 5\}$

2)   Union of two events:

The event $C = A \cup B$ contains all elements of set A or of set B or of both. The symbol $\cup$ is used to denote 'union' operation. For example, Let $A = \{1, 2, 3, 4\}$,   B $= \{4, 5, 6, 7\}$ then $C = A \cup B = \{1, 2, 3, 4, 5, 6, 7\}$

3)   Intersection of two events:

The event C that contains all the elements common to both the events A and B is called the intersection of event A and event B. It is denoted by using the symbol $\cap$. $C = A \cap B$ e.g. Let $A = \{1, 2, 3, 4\}$ $B = \{4, 5, 6, 7\}$ then $C = A \cap B = \{4\}$.

4)   Complementation of an event A:

The event C that contains all the elements of sample space that are not the elements of the event A is called the Complement of event A. It is denoted by $\overline{A}$ or A' i.e. $C = $ or $\overline{A}$ or A'. For example, let a universal set S be 'single digit number', $S = \{0, 1, 2, 3, 4, 5, 6, 7, 8, 9\}$ Let Set $A = \{2, 3, 4\}$ then $A' = \{0, 1, 5, 6, 7, 8, 9\}$.

5)   Event implied by another event:

Let S be a sample space of a random experiment. Let two events E and F be the outcome of the same experiment. Then E & F are subsets of S. Suppose, the two events E & F are such that set E is a subset of F, i.e. $E \subset F$. It means that the event F occurs whenever the event E occurs. In this case, it is also said that the event E implies the event F.For example, if the event E = set of even number between 1 and 9. The event F = set of single digit numbers, then $E = \{2, 4, 6, 8\}$ and $F = \{0, 1, 2, 3, 4, 5, 6, 7, 8, 9\}$. Hence, the set E is a subset of the set F. i.e. F occurs whenever E occurs; and the set E implies set F.

6)   Set theoretic notations

   a) Event "Not A" $\overline{A}$ *or A' or A^c*

b) Event "A or B" $A \cup B$

c) Event "A and B" $A \cap B$

d) Event "A but not B" $A \cap \bar{B}$

e) Event "neither A nor B" $\bar{A} \cap \bar{B}$

f) "Exactly one of the two events A & B" $(A \cap \bar{B}) \cup (\bar{A} \cap B)$

g) "At least one of the events A or B or C" $A \cup B \cup C$

h) Event consisting of all the elements common to three events A, B & C $A \cap B \cap C$

i) Event "Exactly two of the three events A, B and C"
$$(A \cap B \cap \bar{C}) \cup (A \cap \bar{B} \cap C) \cup (\bar{A} \cap B \cap C)$$

j) Event "A but not B & C" $A \cap \bar{B} \cap \bar{C}$

k) De Morgan's Laws:

   1) $\overline{(A \cup B)} = \bar{A} \cap \bar{B}$

   2) $\overline{(A \cap B)} = \bar{A} \cup \bar{B}$

l) For any two given events A and B $A = (A \cap B) \cup (A \cap B')$

7) Venn Diagram:

Geometrical diagrams are used to represent 'sets'. In this diagram, the universal set (sample space of a random experiment) is represented by a rectangle. Any subset of 'S' i.e. event is represented by a closed figure, usually a circle or an ellipse, lying within the rectangular region. The four basic operations are represented by Venn diagrams as shown below.

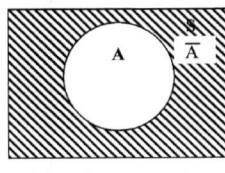

Shaded region represents $\bar{A}$

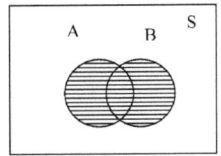

Shaded region represents $A \cup B$

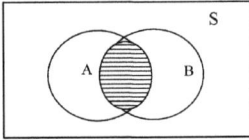

Shaded region represents $A \cap B$

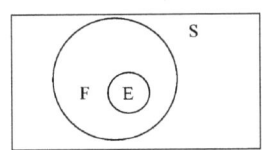

$E \subset F$; E implies F or F is implied by E

8)   Cardinal number or Cardinality of a set:

The number of elements contained in a finite set A is called its Cardinal number or cardinality. It is denoted by n (A). In Venn diagram, the cardinal number of a set is written inside a closed figure representing the set.

For example:

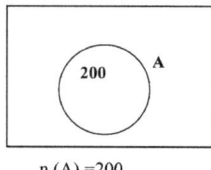

n (A) =200

There are three useful theorems.

1) $n(A \cup B) = n(A) + n(B) - n(A \cap B)$

2)   If the two sets A& B are disjoint (mutually exclusive),

$n (A \cup B) = n (A) + n(B)$

3)   In case of three sets A, B and C

$n (A \cup B \cup C) = n (A) + n(B) + n(C) - n(A \cap B) - n(B \cap C)$

$- n(C \cap A) + n(A \cap B \cap C)$

9) Power Set:

Let A be any set, then the collection of all subsets of A is called the Power set of A and is denoted by P (A).

For example, Let A = {1, 2, 3}.

Then power set of A,

P (A) = {φ, {1, 2, 3}, {1}, {2}, {3}, {1, 2}, {2, 3},{1,3}}

where φ is a null set.

The rule is; if n (A) = n, $n (P (A)) = 2^n$.

Note: It should be noted that symbol P(A) represents the power set of A although the same symbol is used to represent the probability of event A in theory of probability.

10) Ordered pair:

A set A is {1, 2,} and a set B is {a, b, c}.Consider a pair (1, a) such that there is a link from 1 of set A to a of set B; another pair (a,1) such that there is another link from a of set B to 1 of set A. The two pairs are not the same; they are different. Therefore, these are called 'ordered pairs'

11) Cartesian Product:

A Cartesian product of two sets A and B is denoted by A X B. It is a set of all ordered pairs (x, y) such that x is an element of set A and y is an element of set B. Consider set A= {1, 2} and set B = {a, b, c}. A X B = {(1,a), (1,b), (1,c), (2,a), (2,b), (2,c)}. Thus a Cartesian product A X B = {(x, y): where x is an element of set A and y is an element of set B}. The number of elements of a power set A X B is equal to m x n; m is the number of elements of set A and n is that of set B.

12) Relations and Functions:

A relation set R from set A to set B is a set of ordered pairs (x, y) such that x is an element of set A and y is an element of set B; and there is a well-defined link from x to y. This is denoted by (A R B). A relation set (A R B) is a subset of the power set of Cartesian product A X B. That is (A R B) is a subset of P (A X B). The number of elements of set A is m, and that of set B is n. The total number of possible relations from set A to set B is equal to n (P (A X B)). It is equal to (2^{mn})

The domain of the relation (A R B) is the set of x, the first element of ordered pairs (x, y). It is a subset of set A. The co domain is set B; and the range is the set of y, the second element of ordered pairs (x, y). It is a subset of set B.

A relation set F from set A to set B is a function from set A to set B if every element of set A has one and only one image in set B. In other words, every element x of set A has the defined relation with one and only one element y of set B. The domain of function F from set A to set B is set A. The range is a subset of set B.

In probability theory, a real valued function, called a random variable, plays an important role. It is called a real valued function, as its range is a subset of a set of real numbers.

The number of possible binary functions from set A to set B is equal to n^m. The set A has m elements and set B has n elements.

Example: Write a set of all possible relations from set A = {1, 2} to set B = {a, b}

Solution: A X B = { (1,a), (1,b), (2,a),(2,b)};   n(A X B) = m n = 4.

The set of all possible relations = P(AXB) = {Φ, {(1,a)}, {(1,b)}, {(2,a)}, {(2,b)}, {(1,a), (1,b)}, {(1,a), (2,a)}, {(1,a),(2,b)}, {(1,b),(2,a)}, {(1,b),(2,b)}, {(2,a),(2,b)}, {(1,a),(1,b),(2,a)}, {(1,b),(2,a),(2,b)}, {(1,a),(1,b),(2,b)}, {(1,a),(2,b),(2,a)}, {(1,a),(1,b),(2,a),(2,b)}}

The set of all possible binary functions = {{(1,a), (2,a)}, {(1,a),(2,b)}, {(1,b), (2,a)},{(1,b),(2,b)}}

The number of all possible binary functions is equal to $n^m = 2^2 = 4$.

Chapter 4

EVENTS & THEIR PROBABILITIES

1) Simple and Complex events

An event is a subset of a Sample space S of a random experiment. An event is a simple event if it contains only one sample point. A Complex event is an event that can be decomposed into a number of simple events.

Example: Experiment- 'Throwing a die'.

Simple event (A) - 'Getting number 2'

Sample space S = {1, 2, 3, 4, 5, 6}

Therefore, Event A = {2}

'Getting an even number' is say event B. Therefore event B = {2, 4, 6} It is a complex event, can be decomposed as simple events B1 = {2}, B2 = {4}, B3 = {6}. Event B = {2} ∪ {4} ∪ {6}. i.e. B = B1 ∪ B2 ∪ B3.

2) Mutually Exclusive events

Two events A and B, associated with a random experiment, are said to be mutually exclusive if the occurrence of one prevents the occurrence of the other. They do not have any common element or

A∩B = φ = null set. The two sets representing two mutually exclusive events are disjoint sets.

Example: Experiment- 'Throwing a die'.

Event A - 'Getting an even number'

A = {2, 4, 6}

Event B - 'Getting an odd number'

B = {1, 3, 5}

Now, since A ∩ B = { } = φ, A and B are mutually exclusive events.

3) Exhaustive events

A set of events A, B, C... is said to be exhaustive if A ∪ B ∪ C ∪... = S. A set of events is exhaustive if it includes all the sample points of a sample space.

Example:

A card is drawn from a set of 10 cards numbered 1 to 10. Consider two events, event A – 'Even numbered card is drawn' & event B – 'Odd numbered card is drawn'. The set of two events A & B is exhaustive as $A \cup B = S$.

S = {1, 2, 3, 4, 5, 6, 7, 8, 9, 10}
A = {2, 4, 6, 8, 10}
B = {1, 3, 5, 7, 9}

4) Independent events

Two events are said to be independent, if the occurrence of any one of them does not, in any way, affect the probability of occurrence of the other. Suppose the events E & F are independent, then P (E ∩ F) = P (E) X. P (F),

5) Dependent events

Two events are said to be dependent if the occurrence or non-occurrence of one event in any trial, affects the probability of occurrence of the other in subsequent trials.

Example:

A bag contains four black and one white balls. One ball is drawn from the bag and the outcome is noted. The ball is replaced back to the bag. A second ball is drawn and the outcome is noted. The two events are, Event A - 'Getting a white ball in the first draw'. Event B - 'Getting a white ball in the second draw'. The two events A and B are independent events. Now consider the same experiment without replacing the ball after the first draw. If the outcome of the first ball is white, the outcome of the second draw is 'no white ball.' i.e. there is no chance of getting a white ball in the second draw. In case the first draw is black ball, there is a chance, (1 in 4), of getting white ball in the second draw. Thus, two events A and B are dependent events in the case where the ball is not replaced after the first draw.

Let us consider one example. Three coins are tossed together. Consider an event E 'Three heads or three tails occur'; another event an event F 'At least two heads occur', and an event G 'At most two heads occur'. There are three pairs of events, (E, F), (E, G), (F, G). Determine, which pairs are dependent, which are independent, which are mutually exclusive and which are mutually exhaustive.

Solution:

S = {HHH, HHT,HTH,HTT, THH, THT,TTH, TTT}
E = {HHH, TTT}
F = {HHH, HHT, HTH, THH}
G = {TTT, TTH, THT, HTT,THH, HTH, HHT}

Consider the pair E, F;

$E \cap F = $ HHH   so, the pair is not mutually exclusive.

$E \cup F$ is not equal to 'S', so the pair is not exhaustive.

P(E)=1/4, P(F)=1/2, and P(E $\cap$ F) = 1/8. Since P(E $\cap$ F) =P(E) XP(F), the pair is independent.

Consider the pair F, G;

$F \cap G$ = {HHT, HTH, THH}

$F \cup G$ = { HHH, HHT,HTH,THH, TTT,TTH,THT,HTT} = S.

The pair is mutually exhaustive but not exclusive.

P(F) =4/8, P(G)=7/8

P(F $\cap$ G) = 3/8

As P(F $\cap$ G) is not equal to P(F) X P(G), F and G are dependent.

Consider the pair E, G;

$E \cap G = $ TTT   so the pair is not mutually exclusive.

$E \cup G$ = S, so the pair is exhaustive.

P(E) X P(G) =2/8 X 7/8 = 7/32 and P(E $\cap$ G) = 1/8,

Therefore, the pair is dependent.

6)   Equiprobable events

Let events A, B, C and D be four equally likely and mutually exclusive and exhaustive events. i.e. P (A) = P(B) = P(C) = P(D) = p

Let the Sample space S = {A, B, C, D}

i.e.   P(A) + P(B) + P(C) + P(D) = 1 = P(S).

Therefore $4p$ =1 & $p = \dfrac{1}{4}$

In case of a throw of unbiased die, all the six possible outcomes are equally probable or are equiprobable events. Similarly in case of a good toss of a fair coin, the two outcomes Head or Tail are equiprobable events.

7)   Sure and Impossible events

The probability of sure event is one. The probability of impossible events is zero. The probability of any event E lies in a closed interval 0 to 1, i.e. $0 \le P (E) \le 1$.

Example: Event A 'Getting number 10' in a random experiment of 'Throwing a die' is an impossible event. P (A) = zero. Consider event B, associated with the same experiment, 'Getting a number greater than 0 and less than 7' P (B) = one. It is a sure event.

8)   Conditional Probability

Let event E and F be two events associated with the same random experiment. The conditional probability of occurrence of the event E under the condition that event F has occurred is denoted by P(E/F) and is given by:

$$P(E/F) = \frac{P(E \cap F)}{P(F)} \quad \text{provided } P(F) \neq 0.$$

If the two events E &F are independent events then,

$$P(E \cap F) = P(E) \times P(F)$$

In case of dependent events,

$$P(E \cap F) = P(E).P(E/F)$$

Example:

Consider the random experiment of throwing a pair of dice. Let E be the event that 'the sum of the numbers obtained is 10. Let F be the event of 'getting even number on the first die.' Suppose F has already occurred then find the probability of getting the event E.

Solution:

The Sample space has 36 sample points. i.e. n(S) = 36

$S = \{(1,1),(1,2),....(1,6); (2,1),(2,2).....(2,6); (3,1)...(6,1),(6,2), ...(6,6)\}$

$E = \{(4,6),(5,5),(6,4)\}$;   n(E) =3.

$F = \{(2,1),(2,2).....(2,6); (4,1), ...(4,6); (6,1),...(6,6)\}; n(F) = 6 \times 3 = 18$

$E \cap F = \{(4,6), (6,4)\}$ n(E $\cap$ F) =2

Therefore, $P(E/F) = \frac{P(E \cap F)}{P(F)} = \frac{n(E \cap F)/n(S)}{n(F)/ n(S)} = \frac{n(E \cap F)}{n(F)}$

Hence, $P(E/F) = \frac{2}{18} = \frac{1}{9}$

Another definition of conditional probability is $P(B/A) = \frac{m1}{n1}$

Where '*n1*' is the number of elements of the event A and '*m1*' of which are favourable to the event B.

In the example given above $n1 = n(F) = 18$ and two outcomes of the event F, $\{(4,6),(6,4)\}$ is favourable to the event E. Therefore, $m1 = 2$. Hence $P(E/F) = 1/9$

9) Properties of Conditional Probability

1. S a sample space of a random experiment and an event E is its subset $P(S/S) = P(E/E) = P(S/E) = $ one.

2. Set A, set B are events of a sample space S. Set F is an event of S such that $P(F)$ is not equal to zero.

    $P((A \cup B) / F) = P(A/F) + P(B/F) - P((A \cap B)/F)$

3. $P(E'/F) = 1 - P(E/F)$

10) Theorem of Compound Probability

If the probability of an event A happening as a result of a trial is $P(A)$, and after A has happened the probability of an event B happening as a result of another trial is $P(B/A)$, then the probability of both the events A & B happening as a result of two trials is $P(AB)$. The Compound probability is denoted by $P(AB)$ and is equal to $P(A) \times P(B/A)$

Where as $P(B/A)$ is a conditional probability. It is defined as $P(B/A) = \dfrac{m1}{n1}$,

where n1 are the total number of outcomes of the second trial under the condition that the outcome of the first trial is favourable to event A ; m1 outcomes of n1 are favourable to the event B.

Example:

Two cards are drawn from a pack of 52 cards. Find the chance that the first card is king and the second is a queen if the card is not replaced.

Event A of first trial – Drawing a King.

Event B of the second trial – Drawing a Queen.

Two trials are done in succession. A = {Spade King, Heart King,

Diamond King, Club King} $P(A) = \dfrac{4}{52} = \dfrac{1}{13}$

Since first card drawn is not replaced, the sample space of the second experiment has 51 sample points, as out of 52 cards one King is drawn out.

B = {Spade Queen, Heart Queen, Diamond Queen, Club Queen}

Therefore, $P(B/A) = \dfrac{m_1}{n_1} = \dfrac{4}{51}$

$$P(AB) = P(A) \times P(B/A) = \frac{4}{52} \times \frac{4}{51} = \frac{4}{663}$$

11) Inverse Probability

An event A corresponds to a number of exhaustive events B_1, B_2, B_3... B_n. Suppose, probability of event B_i i.e. $P(B_i)$, is given and also the probability of event A under the condition that B_i has occurred, i.e. $P(A/B_i)$, is given. The Baye's Theorem states that $P(B_i/A)$ i.e. the probability of event B_i under the condition that A has occurred or probability that A corresponds to the event B_i is given by:

$$P(Bi\ /\ A) = \frac{P(Bi).P(A/Bi)}{\sum P(Bi).P(A/Bi)}$$

Example:

Three machines M_1, M_2 and M_3 produce identical items. 5%, 4% and 3% items of their respective outputs are faulty. On a certain day M_1 has produced 25%, M_2 has produced 30% of the total output, and the machine M3 has produced the remaining output. An item selected at random is found to be faulty. What is the chance that it is produced by the machine with the highest output?

The output of the 3 machines are 25%, 30% and 100 - (25+30) = 45%. The machine M_3 is the machine with highest output. The question is to find the value of $P(B_3 \backslash A)$.

Event A is 'Drawn item is faulty.'

Event B_i is 'Item is produced by i'th machine M_i'

Given: $P(B_1) = 0.25$, $P(B_2) = 0.30$ and $P(B_3) = 0.45$

Also $P(A/B1) = 0.05$, $P(A/B2) = 0.04$ and $P(A/B3) = 0.03$

Using the formula,

$$P(B_3\ /\ A) = \frac{P(B_3).P(A/B_3)}{\sum P(Bi).P(A/Bi)}$$

$$P(B3\ /\ A) = \frac{0.45 \times 0.03}{0.25 \times 0.05 + 0.30 \times 0.04 + 0.45 \times 0.03}$$

$$= \frac{135}{380} = \frac{27}{76}$$

$$\therefore \text{ The answer is } \frac{27}{76}$$

<u>Note 1</u>: The events B_1, B_2, B_3 form a set of mutually exclusive and exhaustive events.

<u>Note 2</u>: The probabilities $P(B_1)$, $P(B_2)$,...... are called apriori probabilities. These are already known before conducting the experiment.

<u>Note 3</u>: The probabilities $P(A/B_i)$ are known as likelihood probabilities as they tell us how likely the event A under consideration occurs.

<u>Note 4</u>: The probabilities $P(B_i/A)$ are called 'posterior probabilities' as they are determined after conducting the experiment.

Chapter 5

COMBINATORIAL MATHEMATICS

In case of complex problems on probability of Compound events, it is not easy to determine the number of favourable outcomes. Combinatorial Mathematics deals with different ways of determining or counting the number of ways an event can take place.

1)   Multiplication Principle (MP)

If one event can occur in 'm' different ways, a second event in 'n' different ways and third in 'p' different ways and so on, for a finite number of independent events, then the total number of ways in which all events can occur in succession is given by m X n X p X........

Example:

There are three routes from place A to place B. There are two routes from place B to C. How many different routs are there from the place A to the place C?

Solution :

Event 'E$_1$' – 'Route from A to B'   n(E$_1$) = m = 3.

Event 'E$_2$' – 'Route from B to C'   n(E$_2$) = n = 2.

Event 'E$_1$' and Event 'E$_2$' are independent events and they occur in succession to go from A to B to C. Thus, event E is route from A to B to C. Event E = E$_1$ ∩ E$_2$. n(E) = n(E$_1$) X n(E$_2$)

Therefore, n(E) = 3 X 2 = 6.

Answer is 6.

Alternative solution:-

In the following figure, the three routes from A to B are marked as 1, 2 and 3. The routes from B to C are marked as 4 & 5. The possible routes from A to B to C are *a)* 1& 4, *b)* 1& 5, *c)* 2& 4, *d)* 2& 5, *e)* 3& 4 and *f)* 3& 5. Thus, there are six possible routes from A to C.

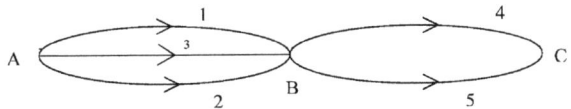

2) Addition Principle

This principle is used to find out the number of ways for at least one event to occur from a set of mutually exclusive events E_1, E_2, E_3... Ek

where $k \geq 1$. Let the event be E such that,

$E = E_1 \cup E_2 \cup E_3 \cup \ldots\ldots\ldots \cup E_k$.

And $n(E) = n(E1) + n(E2) + \ldots\ldots\ldots + n(E_k)$

(Since the events E_1, E_2 etc. are mutually exclusive)

Example:

How many numbers can be formed by using the digits 1, 2 and 3? The repetition of digits is not allowed.

Solution:

Event E_1- 'Single digit number using 1, 2, or 3' i.e. $E_1 = \{1, 2, 3\}$ Event E_2 - 'Two-digit number using 1, 2, and 3' $E_2 = \{12, 13, 21, 23, 31, 32\}$ Event E_3 – 'Three- digit number using 1, 2, and 3' $E_3 = \{123, 132, 231, 213, 312, 321\}$

Now E1, E2 & E3 are mutually exclusive events & $E = E1 \cup E2 \cup E3$

Therefore, $n(E) = n(E1) + n(E2) + n(E3) = 3 + 6 + 6 = 15$.

Ans.: Fifteen numbers can be formed. They are $\{1, 2, 3, 12, 13, 21, 23, 31, 32, 123, 132, 231, 213, 312, 321\}$

3) Combination Principle

The number of all possible different groups of 'r' things selected from a group of 'n' distinct things is denoted by ^nCr.   By definition,

$$^nCr = \frac{n!}{(n-r)!\ r!} = \frac{n\ (n-1)(n-2)\ldots\ldots\ldots2 \times 1}{[(n-r)(n-r-1)(n-r-2)\ldots\times 2 \times 1]\ [r(r-1)\ldots \times 2 \times 1]}$$

Example:

How many different sets of two students can be chosen out of 6 students to represent a school in a mathematical contest?

Solution

Let the students be numbered as 1, 2, 3, 4, 5 & 6. Therefore $n = 6$. Group of 2 students, so $r = 2$. Substituting in the formula,

$$^nCr = \frac{n!}{(n-r)!\, r!} = \frac{6!}{(6-2)!\, X\, 2!} = \frac{6\, X\, 5\, X\, 4\, X\, 3\, X\, 2\, X\, 1}{4\, X\, 3\, X\, 2\, X\, 1\, X\, 2\, X\, 1} = 15$$

Answer = 15 groups i.e. 15 ways in which a group of two students can be formed from 6 students.

Alternative solution:-

Let S = {1, 2, 3, 4, 5, 6} = Set of students.

E = Group of two students.

E = {(1,2), (1,3), (1,4), (1,5), (1,6), (2,3), (2,4), (2,5), (2,6),

(3,4), (3,5), (3,6), (4,5), (4,6), (5,6)}

n(E) = 15.

4) Permutation Principle

The dictionary meaning of permutation is rearranging the order of a set of things. In Mathematics, a permutation is defined as an arrangement of all or part of the elements of a given set in a definite order. The number of possible permutations (arrangements) of 'r' elements taken from a set of 'n' elements is denoted by ^nP_r and is

defined by $^nP_r = \dfrac{n!}{(n-r)!}$

Permutations involve two independent events:

Event 'E$_1$'- selecting a group of 'r' elements from a set of 'n' elements. Event 'E$_2$'- rearranging each group of 'r' elements in all possible ways.

n(E$_1$) = No. of elements of event E$_1$

$$= {}^nC_r = \frac{n!}{(n-r)!\, r!}$$

and   n(E2) = r!

E = E$_1$ ∩ E$_2$

$$\therefore n(E) = n(E_1)\, X\, n(E_2) = \frac{n!}{(n-r)!\, r!}\, X\, r! = \frac{n!}{(n-r)!}$$

Example:

How many 3-digit numbers are possible by using 3-digits 1, 2 and 3 without repetition?

Solution

Possible number of 3-digit numbers are $^nPr \ = \ \dfrac{n!}{(n-r)!}$

Where n = r = 3. $^nPr \ = \ \dfrac{3!}{0!} \ = 3!$

Ans. Possible number of 3-digit numbers are 3! = 6.

Alternatively, let us write a set E of 3-digit numbers using the digits 1, 2, and 3.

E = {123, 132, 231, 213, 312, 321}.

Ans. n(E) = 6.

5) Permutations with repetition allowed

Example:

How many 3-digit numbers can be obtained by using three digits 1, 2 and 3 with repetition of any digit allowed?

Let such set of 3-digit numbers be E.

E= {111, 112, 113, 121, 122, 123, 131, 132, 133, 211, 212, 213, 221, 222, 223, 231, 232, 233, 311, 312, 313, 321, 322, 323, 331, 332, 333}

Thus $n(E) = 3 \times 3 \times 3 \ = \ 3^3 \ = 27$. Therefore, the Ans. is 27. The rule is $n(E) = n^r$ where 'n' is given no. of things and 'r' is number of things in an arrangement with repetition allowed.

Example:

How many two-digit numbers can be found by using 3digits 1, 2 and 3? Repetition of a digit is allowed.

Solution:

n = 3, r =2

Possible 2-digit numbers are $n^r \ = 3^2 \ = 9$

E = {11, 12, 13, 21, 22, 23, 31, 32, 33}

$n(E) = 9 = \ 3^2$

6)   Linear Permutations

Permutation Principle is also used to find out the number of ways in which 'r' vacant spaces in a line, can be filled using elements of a group of 'n' things.

First place can be filled in 'n' ways. Having filled the first place, the second place can be filled in (n-1) ways. The third in (n-2) and so on. So the number.of ways in which 'r' places can be filled

$$= n(n-1)(n-2)........ (n - r + 1) = {}^nPr = \frac{n!}{(n-r)!}$$

7)   Circular Permutation

Arranging 'n' different objects around a circle is called Circular permutation. Consider example of arranging numbers 1, 2, 3, & 4 in a circle. The rule is, number of arrangements = (n-1)!. With n = four, it is equal to 3! i.e. six.

All possible linear arrangements of numbers 1, 2, 3, and 4 are:

1,2,3,4	1,2,4,3	1,3,2,4	1,3,4,2	1,4,2,3	1,4,3,2
2,3,4,1	2,4,3,1	3,2,4,1	3,4,2,1	4,2,3,1	4,3,2,1
3,4,1,2	4,3,1,2	2,4,1,3	4,2,1,3	2,3,1,4	3,2,1,4
4,1,2,3	3,1,2,4	4,1,3,2	2,1,3,4	3,1,4,2	2,1,4,3

Consider each arrangement converted to a circular form. The figure shows two linear arrangements of first column written in circular form. These two circular arrangements are not distinct, as the first circle when rotated through ninety degrees anticlockwise gives the second circle. Therefore, these two are not distinct arrangements. One can easily see that only six arrangements, arranged in a row as shown, are distinct.

Hence, distinct arrangements are six. i.e. (4-1)! Thus, the rule is, the possible number of distinct arrangements of 'n' things around a circle is (n-1)!

Alternate explanation is as follows: There are n numbers of linear distinct arrangements corresponding to a circular arrangement of n distinct elements. For example, a circular arrangement shown in the figure leads to four linear arrangements of the first column. So, x number of distinct circular arrangements of n elements, correspond to n.x linear arrangements. Since linear permutations of n elements is equal to n!; $x = (n! \backslash n) = (n-1)!$

8)   Permutations of 'n' things, which are not distinct

In the total of 'n' things let there be 'p' things identical to one element, 'q' things identical to another element, 'r' things be identical to third element and so on. The permutation

of the 'n' things in this case is given by $\dfrac{n!}{p! x q! x r! \ldots\ldots}$

Example:

In how many ways the letters in the word 'MATHEMATICS' can be arranged?

Solution

Total no. of letters n = 11. The letter 'M' is repeated twice, letter 'A' is repeated twice, 'T' is repeated twice, remaining five letters (H, E, I, C, S) are occurring only once each. Therefore p = 2, q = 2 and r = 2.

$$\text{No. of arrangements} = \frac{11!}{2! \times 2! \times 2!}$$

$$= \frac{11 \times 10 \times 9 \times 8 \times 7 \times 6 \times 5 \times 4 \times 3 \times 2 \times 1}{8}$$

$$= 4158 \times 120 = 498960$$

9)   Permutations with restrictions

Based on given restrictions (one or many) on permutations, a group of permutations is either accepted or rejected from a group of total permutations.

Example:

To form as many as possible 4-digit numbers using digits 0 to 9 without repetition of a digit.

Solution:

Total arrangements of numbers 0 to 9 taken 4 at a time = ^nPr

$= {}^{10}P4 = \dfrac{10!}{6!} = 10 \times 9 \times 8 \times 7 = 5040.$

Out of these, the arrangements with '0' in MSD (most significant digit) place are rejected. Such arrangements are $^9P3$ = 9 X 8 X 7 = 504. Thus the no. of 4-digit numbers possible are = 5040 – 504 = 4536. Therefore, the answer is 4536.

Alternatively, 1000's place i.e. MSD can take any one of nine digits (1 to 9). 100's place can take any one of nine digits including zero and excluding the chosen MSD. 10's place can have any one of eight digits and unit's place can have any one of seven digits. Thus total number of 4-digit numbers possible = 9 X 9 X 8 X 7 = 4536.

Chapter 6

PROBABILITY DISTRIBUTION

1)   Random Variable

A random variable is an event, which is a function from a sample space of a random experiment to a subset of real numbers. It is defined as a real valued function whose domain is a sample space and range is a subset of a set of real numbers. It is denoted by X or X(w), where w is an element of the sample space S. A random variable may be discrete or continuous. Consider an experiment of tossing three coins. Consider a random variable X defined as "the count of tails" The following table shows the function X

S	HHH	HHT	HTH	HTT	THH	THT	TTH	TTT
X	0	1	1	2	1	2	2	3

This an example of discrete random variable

2)   Probability distribution of a discrete random variable

The relation between a random variable X and the corresponding probabilities P(X) is called the probability distribution of the random variable. Let a random variable assume values X_1, X_2, X_3..., Xn with respective probabilities P_1, P_2, P_3... , P_n such that

$P_1 + P_2 + P_3 + ... + P_n = 1$. Like frequency distribution in Statistics, the probability distribution is represented by a table as shown below;

X	X_1	X_2	X_3	....	X_n
P(X)	$P_1 =$	$P_2 =$	$P_3 =$	....	$P_n =$
	$P(X_1)$	$P(X_2)$	$P(X_3)$	....	$P(X_n)$

In statistics, one is familiar with determination of mean, mode, and median, and variance, standard deviation from the frequency distribution. Similarly, these parameters may be calculated using probability distribution. The important parameters are mean value, and the most probable value of the random variable.

Example:

Obtain the probability distribution of the number of heads occurring in a toss of three unbiased coins.

Solution:

Sample space S of the random experiment 'Tossing of three coins' is S = {HHH, HHT, HTH, HTT, THH, THT, TTH, TTT}. The variable X is number of heads. X can take the following values $X_1 = 0$, $X_2 = 1$, $X_3 = 2$ and $X_4 = 3$. The corresponding frequencies are 1, 3, 3 and 1. Since n(S) = 8, $P_1 = \frac{1}{8}$, $P_2 = \frac{3}{8}$, P_3 = and $P_4 = \frac{1}{8}$. Tabular form of distribution is,

X	0	1	2	3
P(X)	1/8	3/8	3/8	1/8

3) Binomial Distribution or Bernoulli Distribution

We come across experiments with only two possible outcomes. For example, 'Quality test of a manufactured item'. The possible outcomes are: 1. an item is defective; or 2. it is non-defective. Secondly, in an experiment 'tossing a coin'. The possible outcomes are 'head' or tail. Such experiments are called Bernoulli or Binomial trials.

In a random experiment of 'tossing a coin', there are only two outcomes 'Head' and 'Tail'. If the experiment is repeated the outcome is always either Head or Tail. Let us consider a random variable X as number of heads in 'n' such trials. The probability of getting Head in any trial is p, and it is equal to $\frac{1}{2}$. The probability of the second event 'Getting Tail' is q and q = 1-p = $1-\frac{1}{2}$. The probability distribution of variable X i.e. the number of Heads in 'n' trials is an example of Binomial Distribution, also called as Bernoulli's distribution after its inventor. In this distribution, the probability P(r) corresponding to X = r is given by the formula.

$P(r) = {}^nCr\ p^r q^{n-r}$

Where, ${}^nCr$ is the number of groups (combinations) of 'n' things taken 'r' at a time and 'n' is the number of independent trials of a random experiment. Each trial's possible outcome is one of the two, (Head or Tail in the above example). 'p' is the probability of one outcome, say 'Head', in a single trial. 'q' is the probability of the other outcome, 'Tail'. Also (p + q) =1; the values of p or q in all the trials are the same. In 'n' trials, 'r' is the number of times the outcome is favourable to the event.

The two constants of binomial distribution are: Mean value = n.p, and the standard deviation = $(npq)^{\frac{1}{2}}$

Let us calculate the binomial distribution corresponding to a random experiment of 'tossing a coin'. Suppose the experiment is repeated four times. Let the number of Heads obtained in four trials be X.

The formula for finding $P(X = r) = {}^nCr\ p^r\ q^{n-r}$ where ${}^nCr = \dfrac{n!}{(n-r)!\,r!}$

$n = 4$, $p = \dfrac{1}{2}$ and $q = \dfrac{1}{2}$;

Therefore, $\quad P(0) = {}^4C_0\, p^0 q^4 \;=\; \dfrac{1}{16}$

$P(1) = {}^4C_1\, p^1 q^{4-1} \;=\; \dfrac{4!}{3! \times 1!} \quad \times (\dfrac{1}{2})^1 \times (\dfrac{1}{2})^{4-1}$

$P(1) = 4 \times \dfrac{1}{2 \times 2 \times 2 \times 2} \;=\; \dfrac{1}{4}$

$P(2) = {}^4C_2\, p^2 q^2 \;=\; \dfrac{4!}{2! \times 2!} \times (\dfrac{1}{2})^2 \times (\dfrac{1}{2})^2 \;=\; \dfrac{4 \times 3 \times 2 \times 1}{2 \times 2} X \dfrac{1}{16}$

$P(2) = \dfrac{3}{8}$

$P(3) = {}^4C_3\, p^3 q^1 \;=\; \dfrac{4!}{3! \times 1!} \times (\dfrac{1}{2})^4 \;=\; \dfrac{4}{16} = \dfrac{1}{4}$

$P(4) = {}^4C_4\, p^4 q^0 \;=\; \dfrac{4!}{4! \times 0!} \times (\dfrac{1}{2})^4 \times 1 \;=\; \dfrac{1}{16}$

X = r	0	1	2	3	4
P(X=r)	1/16	1/4	3/8	1/4	1/16

This table represents the Binomial Distribution function.

The formula $P(X = r) = {}^nCr\, p^r q^{n-r}$ is useful in case of experiments which satisfy the following conditions:

1)   The number of trials i.e. repetitions of a random experiment is finite.

2)   In every trial called Bernoulli's trial there are only two possible outcomes. e.g. success or failure, Head or Tail, Defective or not defective etc.

3)   The trials are independent.

4)   The probability of an outcome is the same in all the trials.

Example

A die is thrown 10 times. If getting an even number is a success; determine the probability of 1) at least 6 successes and 2) at most 5 successes.

<u>Solution:</u>

Given: n=10, the event is 'success if the number is even'. The probability 'p' of getting success in a trial is obtained as follows. The sample space of a trial is S = 1, 2, 3, 4, 5, 6. Out of six total outcomes 3 are favourable to the event 'success'. Thus p = 3/6 = 1/2. The probability 'q' of 'not success or failure' is 1-p = 1- 1/2 =

1/2. Let the event E be 'getting at least six successes'. Therefore, P (E) = P(X = 6) + P(X = 7) + P(X = 8) + P(X = 9) + P(X = 10)

Using binomial distribution formula,

$$P(6) = {}^{10}C_6 p^6 q^{10-6} \quad = \quad \frac{10!}{6! \times 4!} \times (\frac{1}{2})^{10}$$

$$= \quad \frac{10 \times 9 \times 8 \times 7 \times 6!}{6! \times 4 \times 3 \times 2 \times 1} \times (\frac{1}{2})^{10}$$

$$P(6) \quad = \quad 210 \times (\frac{1}{2})^{10}$$

$$P(7) \quad = \quad \frac{10!}{7! \times 3!} \times (\frac{1}{2})^{10} = 120 \times (\frac{1}{2})^{10}$$

$$P(8) \quad = \quad \frac{10!}{8! \times 2!} \times (\frac{1}{2})^{10} = 45 \times (\frac{1}{2})^{10}$$

$$P(9) \quad = \quad \frac{10!}{9! \times 1!} \times (\frac{1}{2})^{10} = 10 \times (\frac{1}{2})^{10}$$

$$P(10) = \quad \frac{10!}{10! \times 0!} \times (\frac{1}{2})^{10} = (\frac{1}{2})^{10}$$

Therefore, $P(E) = (\frac{1}{2})^{10} \ (210 + 120 + 45 + 10 + 1)$

$$= \frac{386}{2^{10}} = \frac{193}{512}$$

Ans. 1) the probability of at least 6 successes is $\frac{193}{512}$

Now consider the second event A = At most 5 successes

$$P(A) = P(X = 0) + P(X = 1) + P(X = 2) + P(X = 3)$$
$$+ P(X = 4) + P(X = 5)$$

Since P(A) + P(E) = 1,   P(A) = 1- P(E)

$$= 1 - \frac{193}{512} = \frac{319}{512}$$

Ans. 2) the probability of 'at most 5 successes' is $\frac{319}{512}$

4)   Poisson distribution

It is a distribution related to the probabilities of events which are extremely rare, but which have a large number of independent opportunities for occurrence. It is a limiting case of Binomial distribution where 'n' is very large 'p' is very small, keeping 'np' fixed equal to 'm' (say). The probability P(r) of 'r' successes in 'n' trials with limiting case of $n \to \infty, p \to 0 \ \& \ m = np$, $p(r) = \frac{m^r}{r!} e^{-m}$

The two constants are : The Mean value = m; and the standard deviation = $m^{\frac{1}{2}}$.

Example

If the probability of a bad reaction from a certain injection is 0.001, determine the chance that out of 2000 individuals more than 2 will get a bad reaction.

Solution:

Since the probability is very small, Poisson distribution applies. The event E is 'More than 2 will get bad reaction.' The random variable X is the number of individuals getting bad reaction.

$P(E) = 1 - [P(0) + P(1) + P(2)]$

Now,   n = 2000, p =0.001. Therefore, np = 2 = m

$P(r) = \dfrac{m^r}{r!} e^{-m}$

$P(0) = \dfrac{2^0 e^{-2}}{0!} = e^{-2}$

$P(1) = \dfrac{2^1 e^{-2}}{1!} = 2e^{-2}$

$P(2) = \dfrac{2^2 e^{-2}}{2!} = 2e^{-2}$

$P(E) = 1 - e^{-2}(1 + 2 + 2) = 1 - 5e^{-2} = 0.32$

Ans. Probability that more than two will get bad reaction is 0.32.

5)   Probability Density Distribution

In case of a continuous random variable, the probability distribution is continuous, (the value of 'n' is infinitely large); and the original definition of probability is not useful. The probability density f(x) of a continuous variable 'x' is such that the probability of x falling in the interval x-½dx to x+½dx is f(x)dx. Also the probability that the variable 'x' lies between two values x1 and x2 is given by $\int_{x_1}^{x_2} f(x)dx$. The range of variable 'x' can be finite or infinite. In case of finite range say a≤ x≤ b, f(x) = $\Phi(x)$. It is a practice to consider f(x) = 0 for values of x outside this range i.e. f(x) = 0 for x < a and f(x) = 0 for x >b. It should be noted that f(x) ≥ 0 and = $\int_{-\infty}^{+\infty} f(x)dx = 1$

6)   Normal Curve

Any quantity whose variation depends on random causes is distributed according to the normal law. The dictionary meaning of the word 'Random' is 'haphazard' or 'unruly'. In case of random experiments, 'random' means without any bias or under some uncontrolled factors. Large number of variables in practice is such that their distribution approximates to the 'Normal Curve'.

The normal curve is the limiting case of the binomial discrete distribution where 'n' is infinitely large and p or q is not very small. The mathematical definition of the normal law is,

$$y = \frac{1}{\sqrt{2\pi}}.e^{-z^2/2}, \text{ where } z \text{ is a normal variate.}$$

A typical normal curve is shown in the figure. The tables are available giving area

$$= \int_0^z \frac{1}{\sqrt{2\pi}}.e^{-z^2/2} dz \text{ for values of 'z' ranging from 0.00 to 3.19. The following properties}$$

of normal curve are important.

i.   Maximum ordinate is equal to $\dfrac{1}{\sqrt{2\pi}}$ It occurs at z = 0.

ii.   The curve is bell shaped and is symmetrical about Y-axis.

iii. Total area under the curve i.e. $= \int_{-\infty}^{+\infty} ydz = 1$

iv. $\int_{-1}^{+1} ydz = 0.6827$ i.e. 68.27% of total area.

v. $\int_{-2}^{+2} ydz = 0.9544$ i.e. 95.44% of total area.

vi. $\int_{-3}^{+3} ydz = 0.9973$ i.e. 99.73% of total area.

vii. $\int_{-z}^{+z} ydz = 0.5$ for z = 0.67.

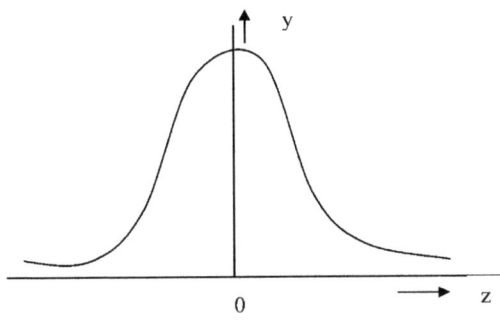

A Typical Normal Curve

z	0	1	2	3	4	5	6	7	8	9
0	0	0.004	0.008	0.012	0.016	0.0199	0.0239	0.0279	0.0319	0.035
0.1	0.0398	0.0438	0.0478	0.0517	0.0557	0.0596	0.0636	0.0675	0.0714	0.0754
0.2	0.0793	0.0832	0.0871	0.091	0.0948	0.0987	0.1026	0.1064	0.1103	0.1141
0.3	0.1179	0.1217	0.1255	0.1293	0.1331	0.136	0.1406	0.1443	0.148	0.1517
0.4	0.1554	0.1591	0.1628	0.1664	0.17	0.1736	0.1772	0.1808	0.1844	0.1879
0.5	0.1915	0.195	0.1985	0.2019	0.2054	0.2088	0.2123	0.2157	0.219	0.2224
0.6	0.2258	0.2291	0.2324	0.2357	0.2389	0.2422	0.2454	0.2486	0.2518	0.2549
0.7	0.258	0.2612	0.2642	0.2673	0.2704	0.2734	0.2764	0.2794	0.2823	0.2852
0.8	0.2881	0.291	0.2939	0.2967	0.2996	0.3023	0.3051	0.3078	0.3106	0.3133
0.9	0.3159	0.3186	0.3212	0.3238	0.3264	0.3289	0.3315	0.334	0.3365	0.3389
1	0.3413	0.3438	0.3461	0.3485	0.3508	0.3531	0.3554	0.3577	0.3599	0.3621
1.1	0.3643	0.3665	0.3686	0.3708	0.3729	0.3749	0.377	0.379	0.381	0.383
1.2	0.3849	0.3869	0.3888	0.3907	0.3925	0.3944	0.3962	0.398	0.3997	0.4015
1.3	0.4032	0.4049	0.4066	0.4082	0.4099	0.4115	0.4131	0.4147	0.4162	0.4177
1.4	0.4192	0.4207	0.4222	0.4236	0.4251	0.4265	0.4279	0.4292	0.4306	0.4319
1.5	0.4332	0.4345	0.4357	0.437	0.4382	0.4394	0.4406	0.4418	0.4429	0.4441
1.6	0.4452	0.4465	0.4474	0.4484	0.4495	0.4505	0.4515	0.4525	0.4535	0.4545
1.7	0.4554	0.4564	0.4573	0.4582	0.4591	0.4599	0.4608	0.4616	0.4625	0.4633
1.8	0.4641	0.4649	0.4656	0.4664	0.4671	0.4678	0.4686	0.4693	0.4699	0.4706
1.9	0.4713	0.4719	0.4726	0.4732	0.4738	0.4744	0.475	0.4756	0.4761	0.4767
2	0.4772	0.4778	0.4783	0.4788	0.4793	0.4798	0.4803	0.4808	0.4812	0.4817
2.1	0.4821	0.4826	0.483	0.4834	0.4838	0.4842	0.4846	0.485	0.4854	0.4857
2.2	0.4861	0.4864	0.4868	0.4871	0.4875	0.4878	0.4881	0.4884	0.4887	0.489
2.3	0.4893	0.4896	0.4898	0.4901	0.4904	0.4906	0.4909	0.4911	0.4913	0.4916
2.4	0.4918	0.492	0.4922	0.4925	0.4927	0.4929	0.4931	0.4932	0.4934	0.4936
2.5	0.4938	0.494	0.4941	0.4943	0.4945	0.4946	0.4948	0.4949	0.4951	0.4952
2.6	0.4953	0.4955	0.4956	0.4957	0.4959	0.496	0.4961	0.4962	0.4963	0.4964
2.7	0.4965	0.4966	0.4967	0.4968	0.4969	0.497	0.4971	0.4972	0.4973	0.4974
2.8	0.4974	0.4975	0.4976	0.4977	0.4977	0.4978	0.4979	0.4979	0.498	0.4981
2.9	0.4981	0.4982	0.4982	0.4983	0.4984	0.4984	0.4985	0.4985	0.4986	0.4986
3	0.4987	0.4987	0.4987	0.4988	0.4988	0.4989	0.4989	0.4989	0.499	0.499
3.1	0.499	0.4991	0.4991	0.4991	0.4992	0.4992	0.4992	0.4992	0.4993	0.4993

Table 1: Area under the normal curve, (from zero to z)

7)   Normal Continuous Probability distribution

In case of a continuous random variable 'X' we consider the probability density function f(x), such that the probability that the variable X is fully within the interval $(x - \frac{1}{2}dx)$ to $(x + \frac{1}{2}dx)$ is $f(x)dx$:

The Cumulative probability distribution function

$$F(x) = P(X \leq x) = \int_{-\infty}^{x} f(x)dx$$

In a limiting case of a binomial distribution function (discrete) with 'n' infinitely large & 'p' is not very small, the probability that the variate 'x' lies between two values x_1 and x_2, $(x_1 \leq x \leq x_2)$, is given by $P(x_1 \leq x \leq x_2) = \frac{1}{\sigma\sqrt{2\pi}} \int_{x_1}^{x_2} e^{-(x-\mu)^2/2\sigma^2} dx$

Let $z = \frac{x - \mu}{\sigma}$, μ is the mean and sigma is the standard variation of X.

Then, $P(z_1 \leq z \leq z_2) = \int_{z_1}^{z_2} \frac{1}{\sqrt{2\pi}} \cdot e^{-z^2/2} dz$

The function $\frac{1}{\sqrt{2\pi}} e^{-z^2/2}$ represents a normal curve or 'z' is a normal variate. The table and all the properties of normal curve are applicable.

Example:

In a test on 2000 electric bulbs, it was found that the life of a particular make was normally distributed with an average life (μ) of 2040 hours and SD (σ) of 60 hours. Estimate the number of bulbs likely to burn for (a) more than 2150 hrs. (b) Less than 1950 hrs and (c) between 1950 and 2150 hrs.

Solution

Given X = Random variable = Life of a bulb in number of hours

$\mu = 2040$ & $\sigma = 60$

Normal variable $z = \frac{x - \mu}{\sigma} = \frac{2150 - 2040}{60} = 1.83$

The probability P(X > 2150) that life is more than 2150 hours is equal to the area of the normal curve to the right of the ordinate at z = 1.83. From the table, the area A corresponding to z = 1.83 is 0.4664

∴ P(X > 2150) = 0.5 – 0.4664 = 0.0336

= 3.36%

Now, N = 2000 bulbs.

a)   ∴ No. of bulbs likely to burn for more than 2150 hrs is equal to

$$2000 \times \frac{3.36}{100} \cong 67 \text{ bulbs.}$$

b)   No. of bulbs likely to burn for less than 1950 hrs

= 2000 X Area (B) of normal curve to the left of the ordinate z.

$$\text{Where, } z = \frac{-(2040-1950)}{60} = \frac{-90}{60} = -1.5$$

Since the curve is symmetrical & area A between Y axis and the ordinate z = 1.5 as given by the table is 0.4332, B = 0.5 – 0.4332 = 0.0668

∴ Ans. = 2000 X 0.0668 = 133.6 ≅ 134 bulbs

c)   No. of bulbs with life between 1950 and 2150

= 2000 {1 – (P(X<1950) + P (X > 2150))}

= 2000 [1- (0.0668 + 0.0336)]

= 2000 X 0.8996 = 1799 (approx.)

Ans. 1799 bulbs with life between 1950 and 2150 hrs.

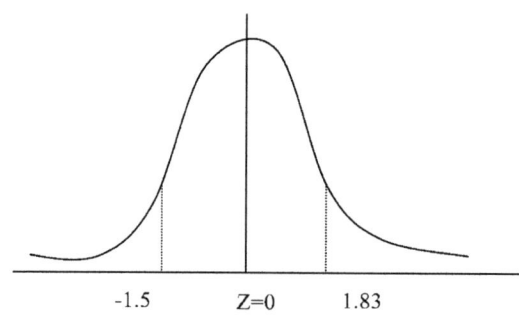

-1.5   Z=0   1.83

8) **Probable Error**

Any lot of articles manufactured to certain specification is subject to random or uncontrollable error. In addition, measurement of any physical quantity is subjected to random error. The error value is small, unpredictable and varies irregularly from one trial to another so the errors follow a normal distribution. Frequently used specification of random error is the 'probable error'. It is defined as error λ such that the probability of the error falling within μ-λ and μ+λ is exactly equal to 1/2 and is also equal to the chance of an error falling outside these limits. 'μ' is the mean error and is equal to zero in case of measurement free of any systematic error. Since

the curve is symmetrical and $\mu = 0$, $\displaystyle\int_{0}^{\lambda/\sigma} \frac{1}{\sqrt{2\pi}} \cdot e^{-z^2/2} dz = \frac{1}{4}$

From the Table, z = 0.6745 corresponding to P(z) = 0.25.

Thus the probable error λ for $\mu = 0$ is $\lambda = 0.6745$ X σ,

σ is the standard deviation.

Chapter 7

EXAMPLES

1) A bag contains 3 white and 2 green balls and another bag contains two white and four green balls. A bag is chosen at random and a ball is drawn from it at random. What is the probability that the ball drawn is white?

Solution:

Two independent experiments, 'a bag is chosen at random' and 'a ball is drawn at random' are carried out in succession. Two outcomes of experiment 1 are {Bag B_1, Bag B_2}. $P(B_1) = P(B_2) = 1/2$. The outcomes of experiment 2 favourable to the event (E) 'the ball drawn is white' are (1) bag B1 is chosen and a white ball is drawn from it. and (2) bag B2 is chosen and a white ball is drawn from it.

$$\therefore P(E) = P(E_1) + P(E_2) = P(B_1)P(W/B_1) + P(B_2)P(W/B_2)$$

$$P(E) = \frac{1}{2} \times \frac{3}{5} + \frac{1}{2} \times \frac{2}{6} = \frac{9+5}{30} = \frac{14}{30} = \frac{7}{15}$$

Ans. $P(E) = \dfrac{7}{15}$.

2) A six-faced die is so biased that it is twice likely to show an even number as an odd. It is thrown twice. What is the probability that the sum of the numbers shown is even?

Solution:

Experiment is 'Throwing a biased die'. Two outcomes are

E_1 – 'Showing of an even number', E_2 – 'Showing of an odd number'. It is given that $P(E_1) = 2 P(E_2)$; and since $P(E_1) + P(E_2) = 1$,

$$P(E_2) = 1/3 \text{ and } P(E_1) = 2/3 \dots\dots\dots\dots (1)$$

Consider the event 'E'. 'The sum is even' of the experiment 'two throws of the die.' The event 'E' is the union of two mutually exclusive events A and B. 'Both numbers are even is an event A & 'Both numbers are odd' is an event B'.

Now $P(A) = P(E_1) \times P(E_1)$

$$= \frac{2}{3} \times \frac{2}{3} = \frac{4}{9}$$

$P(B) = P(E_2) \times P(E_2)$

$$= \frac{1}{3} \times \frac{1}{3} = \frac{1}{9}$$

$\therefore P(E) = P(A) + P(B)$

$$= \frac{4}{9} + \frac{1}{9} = \frac{5}{9}$$

Ans. Probability that the sum of the numbers shown is even

$$= \frac{5}{9}.$$

3)   A, B, C toss a coin in that order, the one who tosses the head first wins a prize. Find the respective chance of winning.

Solution:

Experiment is 'A, B, C toss a coin in that order.' The possible outcomes of the experiment are S = {HHH, HHT, HTH, HTT, THH, THT, TTH} The 8th outcome TTT is not included as it is assumed that one of the three wins. [Note: A sample space has the outcomes of the toss of a coin by A, B and C in that order i. e THT denotes that 'A' tossed 'Tail', 'B' tossed 'Head' and 'C' tossed 'Tail'.]

The outcomes of S favourable to event A 'A wins' are (HHH, HHT, HTH, HTT) $\therefore P(A) = \frac{4}{7}$.

Event B: 'B wins' i.e. B throws 'Head' and A does not throw 'Head'.

$\therefore P(B) = \frac{2}{7}$

Event C: 'C wins' i.e. C throws 'Head' but A & B both do not throw

'Head' $\therefore P(C) = \frac{1}{7}$

Ans. $P(A) = \frac{4}{7}$, $P(B) = \frac{2}{7}$ & $P(C) = \frac{1}{7}$

4)   The results after conducting examination in 2 papers A and B for 20 candidates are recorded as follows: 8 candidates passed in paper A, 7 passed in paper B, 8 failed in both papers A and B. If out of these candidates one is selected at random, find the probability that the candidate

i.   Passes in both papers.

ii.   Failed only in A.

iii.   Failed in A or B.

Solution:

Let us draw Venn diagram. Universal set or sample space of 20 candidates is represented by a rectangle. Two intersecting circles represent the two events; event A – Passed in paper A; event B – passed in paper B. Given n(S) = 20, n(A) = 8 and n(B) =7. The shaded area represents the event C – Failed in both A and B. n(C) =8

Area 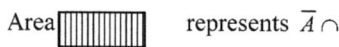   represents $\bar{A} \cap B$

Area   represents $A \cap B$

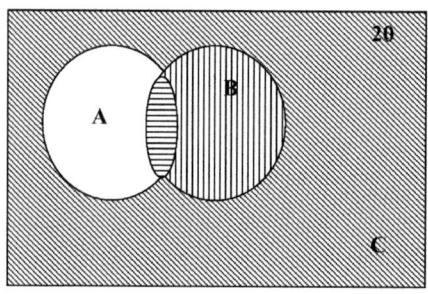

Now $C = \overline{A \cup B}$

n(A $\cup$ B) = n(S) – n(C) = 20 – 8 = 12.

$n(A \cup B) = n(A) + n(B) - n(A \cap B)$

Substituting for n(A $\cup$ B), n(A)& n(B)

12 = 8 + 7 - n(A $\cap$ B)

$\therefore$ n(A $\cap$ B) = 15 – 12 = 3.

Ans. 1 – Passes in both papers = $n(A \cap B) = 3$.

$$P(A \cap B) = \frac{3}{20}$$

Ans. 2 – Failed only in A i.e. $P(A' \cap B)$ failed in A but passed in B.

$$n(A' \cap B) = n(A \cup B) - n(A) = 12 - 8 = 4$$

$$\therefore P(A' \cap B) = \frac{4}{20} = \frac{1}{5}.$$

Ans. 3 – Failed in A or B. i.e. $A' \cup B'$

$$\therefore n(A' \cup B') = n(A \cap B)' = 20\text{-}3 = 17.$$

$$\therefore P(\text{ failed in A or B}) = P(A' \cup B') = \frac{17}{20}$$

Ans. (1) $\frac{3}{20}$, (2) $\frac{1}{5}$ and (3) $\frac{17}{20}$

5)   Find the probability of throwing 17 with a single throw of 3 dice together.

Solution:

    '3 dice throwing together.' In this experiment each one of the 3 dice can have any number from 1 to 6. The possible number of outcomes $n(S) = 6^3 = 216$. Outcomes favourable to the event A 'Total is 17' are all possible permutations of the three numbers 5, 6 and 6. Since 6 is repeated twice.

$$^3P_3 = \frac{3!}{0! \times 2!} = 3 \text{ i.e. (566, 656 and 665)}$$

$$\therefore P(A) = \frac{3}{216} = \frac{1}{72}$$

Ans. $\frac{1}{72}$

6)   The chance that aircraft will return from an operational flight is $\frac{1}{5}$. If 20 aircrafts are engaged in an air raid operation at a time, what is the probability that (a) all of them will return safe. (b) only 15 of them will return safe and (c) at least 15 of them will return safe.

Solution:

    It is a case of Bernoulli's trial with only two possible outcomes (1) will return safely (2) will not return safely. Let 'p' be the probability that an air craft will return safely. p = 1/5. Let 'q' be the probability that an aircraft will not return safely since p + q = 1, q = 1- p = 4/5.

Let X be a random variable denoting the number of aircrafts that return safely. X follows the Binomial distribution.

X = r = 20. n = 20

$$\therefore P(20) = {}^{20}C_{20}\ (\frac{1}{5})^{20} \times (\frac{4}{5})^{20-20} = (\frac{1}{5})^{20}$$

(2) Only 15 of them will return safely. i.e. X = 15

$$\therefore P(15) = {}^{20}C_{15}\ (\frac{1}{5})^{15} \times (\frac{4}{5})^{5}$$

$$= \frac{20!}{15! \times 5!} \times \frac{4^5}{1} \times (\frac{1}{5})^{20}$$

$$= \frac{4^5}{5^{20}} \times \frac{20!}{15! \times 5!}$$

(3) At least 15 of them will return safe – Let this event be E

P(E) = P(X = 15) + P(X = 16) + P(X = 17) + P(X = 18) +
        P(X = 19) + P(X = 20)

$$P(E) = (\frac{1}{5})^{20} \{ {}^{20}C_{15} \times 4^5 + {}^{20}C_{16} \times 4^4 + {}^{20}C_{17} \times 4^3$$

$$+ {}^{20}C_{18} \times 4^2 + {}^{20}C_{19} \times 4^1 + {}^{20}C_{20} \times 4^0\}$$

$$= (\frac{1}{5})^{20} \{1 + 4.\ {}^{20}C_1 + 16.\ {}^{20}C_2 + 64.\ {}^{20}C_3 + 256.\ {}^{20}C_4$$

$$+ 1024.\ {}^{20}C_5\}$$

7.   (a)   What is the probability that a leap year selected at random will contain 53 Sundays?   (b) What is the probability that a non – leap year selected at random will contain 53 Mondays?

Solution

(a) A leap year has 366 days i.e. 52 weeks and 2 days. Let us consider the experiment 'Last two days of the randomly chosen leap year.' The sample space is,

{(Sunday, Monday), (Monday, Tuesday), (Tuesday, Wednesday), (Wednesday, Thursday), (Thursday, Friday), (Friday, Saturday), (Saturday, Sunday)}

Sample points favourable to the event A, '53 Sundays' i.e. the last two days include Sunday, are {(Sunday, Monday), (Saturday, Sunday)}. n(S) = 7 & n(A) = 2.

$$\therefore \text{Probability} = \frac{n(A)}{n(S)} = \frac{2}{7}.$$

(b) In case of non-leap year there are 52 weeks and one day. Last day of the randomly selected non-leap year is one of the 7 days {Sunday, Monday, Tuesday, Wednesday, Thursday, Friday, Saturday}

$\therefore$ The required probability $=\frac{1}{7}$.

8)   Four persons are to be chosen at random from a group containing 3 men, 3 women and four children. Find the probability that exactly two of them will be children?

Solution

Four persons are selected from a group of 10 persons (3 men, 3 women & 4 children). Possible groups i.e. possible combinations are

$$^{10}C_4 = \frac{10!}{6! \times 4!} = \frac{10 \times 9 \times 8 \times 7}{4 \times 3 \times 2 \times 1} = 210 = n(S)$$

An event B is' selecting a group of four persons with exactly two children'. Out of n(S), the favourable sample points i.e. groups of 4 with exactly two children are n(B). 'C' is an event – 'selecting at random, a group of 2 children from a group of 4 children'

$$\therefore n(C) = {}^4C_2 = \frac{4!}{2! \times 2!} = 6.$$

'D' is an event 'selecting at random a group of 2 persons from a group of 3 men and 3 women'.

$$\therefore n(D) = {}^6C_2 = \frac{6!}{2! \times 4!} = \frac{6 \times 5}{2 \times 1} = 15.$$

Since C and D are independent events, Event B = C AND D.

n(B) = n(C) X n(D)   (By Multiplication principle)

= 6 X 15 = 90

$\therefore$ The required probability $= \frac{90}{210} = \frac{3}{7} = n(B)/ n(S)$

9)   A box contains 4 red, 4 white and 5 green balls. 3 balls are drawn together at random from the box. Find the probability that they may be (1) all different   (2) all of the same colour.

Solution

Sample space S = '3 balls are drawn together'

$n(S) = {}^{13}C_3 = \dfrac{13!}{3! \times 10!} = \dfrac{13 \times 12 \times 11}{3 \times 2 \times 1} = 286 \ \ldots\ldots(1)$

1)   'All different' is say event 'A'

It is the event '1 red, 1white, and 1green'

By Multiplication principle,

$n(A) = n(r) \times n(w) \times n(g) = {}^4C_1 \times {}^4C_1 \times {}^5C_1$

$\qquad = 4 \times 4 \times 5 = 80$

$P(A) = \dfrac{n(A)}{n(S)} \quad = \quad \dfrac{80}{286} \ = \ \dfrac{40}{143}$

Ans. Probability that ' All the three balls are different' is $\dfrac{40}{143}$

2)   'All of the same colour' is say event B.

Event B can take place in 3 different ways.

Event B = Event B_1 (All are red) $\cup$ Event B_2 (All are white) $\cup$

Event B_3 (All are green).

B_1, B_2, & B_3 are mutually exclusive. By Addition principle,

$\therefore\ n(B) = n(B_1) + n(B_2) + n(B_3)$

$\qquad = {}^4C_3 + {}^4C_3 + {}^5C_3$

$\qquad = 4 + 4 + 10 = 18$

$\therefore\ P(B) = \dfrac{n(B)}{n(S)} \quad = \quad \dfrac{18}{286} \ = \ \dfrac{9}{143}$

Ans. Probability that 'All the 3balls drawn are of the same colour' is $\dfrac{9}{143}$

10) A bag contains 3 white balls and 4 black balls. Two balls are drawn one by one without replacement. Find the probability that both are white.

Solution

It is a case of compound and conditional probability.

Event A- 'First draw is a white ball'. P(A) = 3/7

Event B- Second draw is a white ball. The probability that the second draw is a white ball, given that the first draw is a white ball is P (B/A).

The sample space of second draw, given the first draw is a white ball is {white, white, black, black, black, black,}; therefore, P (B/A) = 2/6 = 1/3

P (AB) is the probability that both the balls are white,

$$P(AB) = P(A) \times P(B/A) = \frac{3}{7} \times \frac{1}{3} = \frac{1}{7}$$

$$\text{Ans. } P(AB) = \frac{1}{7}.$$

11) A can hit a target 3 times in 6 shots. B can hit the target 2 times in 6 shots and C 4 times in 4 shots. What is the probability that at least two hit the target?

<u>Solution</u>

Event A - 'A hits the target'

$$P(A) = \frac{3}{6} = \frac{1}{2}, \quad P(A') = \frac{1}{2}$$

Similarly, Event B - 'B hits the target'

$$P(B) = \frac{2}{6} = \frac{1}{3}, P(B') = \frac{2}{3}$$

Event C - 'C' hits the target

$$P(C) = \frac{4}{4} = 1 \qquad P(C') = 0$$

Event D – 'Two out of 3 hit the target'

The event D can occur in 3 ways

(i)   A & B hit the target but not C

(ii)   A & C hit the target but not B and

(iii) B &C hit the target but not A

$$\therefore D = A \cap B \cap C' + A \cap B' \cap C + A' \cap B \cap C$$

A, B and C are independent events.

P(D) = P(A). P(B). P(C') + P(A). P(B'). P(C) + P(A'). P(B). P(C)

$$= \frac{1}{2} \times \frac{1}{3} \times 0 + \frac{1}{2} \times \frac{2}{3} \times 1 + \frac{1}{2} \times \frac{1}{3} \times 1$$

$$= 0 + \frac{1}{3} + \frac{1}{6} = \frac{2+1}{6} = \frac{1}{2}$$

Event E – Three out of 3 hit the target

$$P(E) = P(A \cap B \cap C) = \frac{1}{2} \times \frac{1}{3} \times 1 = \frac{1}{6}$$

Event F – At least two out of 3 hit the target.

$$\therefore P(F) = P(D) + P(E) = \frac{1}{2} + \frac{1}{6} = \frac{4}{6} = \frac{2}{3}$$

Ans.   Probability that at least two hit the target = $P(F) = \dfrac{2}{3}$

12) Three cards are drawn successively without replacement from a well-shuffled pack of 52 cards. A random variable 'X' denotes the number of Spades in the three cards. Determine the probability distribution of X.

Solution

 There are 3 draws. Each draw has only two possible outcomes 'Spade' or 'Not spade'. Let us denote the outcomes of the three draws as

$(S_1, \bar{S}_1)$, $(S_2, \bar{S}_2)$ and $(S_3, \bar{S}_3)$.

1st draw $- P(S_1) = \dfrac{13}{52} = \dfrac{1}{4}$; $P(\bar{S}_1) = 1 - \dfrac{1}{4} = \dfrac{3}{4}$

2nd draw $-$ The probabilities are conditional;

$P(S_2/S_1) = \dfrac{12}{51}$, $P(\bar{S}_2/S_1) = \dfrac{39}{51}$; $P(S_2/\bar{S}_1) = \dfrac{13}{51}$, $P(\bar{S}_2/\bar{S}_1) = \dfrac{38}{51}$

3rd draw $-$ The probabilities are conditional.

$P[S_3/(S_2/S_1)] = \dfrac{11}{50}$, $P[\bar{S}_3/(S_2/S_1)] = \dfrac{39}{50}$

$P[S_3/(\bar{S}_2/S_1)] = \dfrac{12}{50}$, $P[\bar{S}_3/(\bar{S}_2/S_1)] = \dfrac{38}{50}$

$P[S_3/(S_2/\bar{S}_1)] = \dfrac{12}{50}$, $P[\bar{S}_3/(S_2/\bar{S}_1)] = \dfrac{38}{50}$

$P[S_3/(\bar{S}_2/\bar{S}_1)] = \dfrac{13}{50}$, $P[\bar{S}_3/(\bar{S}_2/\bar{S}_1)] = \dfrac{37}{50}$

 In case of the 2nd draw, the sample space has 12 or 13 spades depending upon the outcome of the 1st draw. Similarly in case of 3rd draw, the sample space has 13, 12 or 11 spades depending upon the outcomes of 2nd and 1st draws. 'X' is the random variable 'the number of spades in the three cards drawn'. The probability of X is the compound probability.

$$P(X=0) = P(\bar{S}_1).\, P(\bar{S}_2/\bar{S}_1).\, P[\bar{S}_3/(\bar{S}_2/\bar{S}_1)] = P(\bar{S}_1\ \bar{S}_2\ \bar{S}_3)$$

$$\therefore\ P(X{=}0) = \frac{3}{4} \times \frac{38}{51} \times \frac{37}{50} = \frac{703}{1700}$$

$$P(X{=}1) = P(S_1\ \bar{S}_2\ \bar{S}_3) + P(\bar{S}_1 S_2\ \bar{S}_3) + P(\bar{S}_1\ \bar{S}_2 S_3)$$

$$= P(S_1).\, P(\bar{S}_2/S_1).\, P[\bar{S}_3/(\bar{S}_2/S_1)] + P(\bar{S}_1).\, P(S_2/\bar{S}_1).\, P[\bar{S}_3/(S_2/\bar{S}_1)]$$

$$+ P(\bar{S}_1).\, P(\bar{S}_2/\bar{S}_1).\, P[S_3/(\bar{S}_2/\bar{S}_1)]$$

$$P(X{=}1) = \frac{1}{4} \times \frac{39}{51} \times \frac{38}{50} + \frac{3}{4} \times \frac{13}{51} \times \frac{38}{50} + \frac{3}{4} \times \frac{38}{51} \times \frac{13}{50}$$

$$P(X{=}1) = \frac{247}{1700} + \frac{247}{1700} + \frac{247}{1700} = \frac{741}{1700}$$

$$P(X{=}2) = P(\bar{S}_1\ S_2 S_3) + P(S_1\ \bar{S}_2\ S_3) + P(S_1\ S_2\ \bar{S}_3)$$

$$= P[S_3/(S_2/\bar{S}_1)]\ .P(S_2/\bar{S}_1).\, P(\bar{S}_1) + P[S_3/(\bar{S}_2/S_1)]\ .P(\bar{S}_2/S_1).xP(S_1) +$$

$$P[\bar{S}_3/(S_2/S_1)]\ .P(S_2/S_1).\, P(S_1)$$

$$P(X{=}2) = \frac{12}{50} \times \frac{13}{51} \times \frac{3}{4} + \frac{12}{50} \times \frac{39}{51} \times \frac{1}{4}$$

$$+ \frac{39}{50} \times \frac{12}{51} \times \frac{1}{4}$$

$$= \frac{234}{1700}$$

$$P(X{=}3) = P(S_1\ S_2\ S_3) = P(S_1).\, P(S_2/S_1).\, P[S_3/(S_2/S_1)]$$

$$= \frac{1}{4} \times \frac{12}{51} \times \frac{11}{50} = \frac{22}{1700}$$

Ans. Distribution Table

X	0	1	2	3
P(X)	$\frac{703}{1700}$	$\frac{741}{1700}$	$\frac{234}{1700}$	$\frac{22}{1700}$

$$\text{Check}\ \sum_{I=0}^{3} p(x) = \frac{703 + 741 + 234 + 22}{1700} = \frac{1700}{1700} = 1$$

13) A random variable X has the following probability distribution

(i) Find K (ii) Evaluate P(X< 4), P(X≥7), P(2< X< 5).

X	0	1	2	3	4	5	6	7	8
P(X)	K	3K	5K	7K	8K	11K	0	K	3K

Solution

$(i) \sum_{x=0}^{3} p(x) = 1 \quad \therefore K(1 + 3 + 5 + 7 + 8 + 11 + 0 + 1 + 3) = 1$

$\therefore 39K = 1$ or $K = \dfrac{1}{39}$ Ans. $K = \dfrac{1}{39}$

(ii) $P(X< 4) = P(X= 0) + P(X= 1) + P(X= 2) + P(X= 3)$

$\qquad = K(1 + 3 + 5 + 7) = 16 K$

Ans. $P(X< 4) = \dfrac{16}{39}$

$P(X \geq 7) = P(X= 7) + P(X= 8) = 4K$

Ans. $P(X \geq 7) = \dfrac{4}{39}$

$P(2< X< 5) = P(X= 3) + P(X= 4) = 7K + 8K$

Ans. $P(2< X< 5) = \dfrac{15}{39}$

14) Find the probability distribution of the number of white balls drawn when three balls are drawn, one by one without replacement, from a bag containing 4white and 6red balls.

Solution

Let event S be 'Drawing of a white ball.' and S' be 'drawing of a non-white ball'. Since 3 balls are drawn one by one without replacement the sample space of 2nd and 3rd draws are conditional. As the balls are drawn one by one, the probability of drawing a number of white balls is a compound probability following the multiplication rule.

Thus $P(S_1) = \dfrac{4}{10}$, $P(\bar{S}_1) = \dfrac{6}{10}$

$P(S_2/S_1) = \dfrac{3}{9}$, $P(\bar{S}_2/S_1) = \dfrac{6}{9}$, $P(S_2/\bar{S}_1) = \dfrac{4}{9}$ & $P(\bar{S}_2/\bar{S}_1) = \dfrac{5}{9}$

$P[S_3/(S_2/S_1)] = \dfrac{2}{8} = \dfrac{1}{4}$, $P[\bar{S}_3/(S_2/S_1)] = \dfrac{1}{4} \times 3$

$P[S_3/(\bar{S}_2/S_1)] = \dfrac{3}{8}$, $P[\bar{S}_3/(\bar{S}_2/S_1)] = \dfrac{5}{8}$

$P[S_3/(S_2/\bar{S}_1)] = \dfrac{3}{8}$, $P[\bar{S}_3/(S_2/\bar{S}_1)] = \dfrac{5}{8}$

$P[S_3/(\bar{S}_2/\bar{S}_1)] = \dfrac{1}{2}$, $P[\bar{S}_3/(\bar{S}_2/\bar{S}_1)] = \dfrac{4}{8} = \dfrac{1}{2}$

Now X takes the values 0, 1, 2 and 3.

$P(X=0) = P(\bar{S}_1 \bar{S}_2 \bar{S}_3) = P(\bar{S}_1). \ P(\bar{S}_2/\bar{S}_1). \ P[\bar{S}_3/(\bar{S}_2/\bar{S}_1)]$

$P(X=0) = \dfrac{6}{10} \times \dfrac{5}{9} \times \dfrac{4}{8} = \dfrac{1}{6}$

$P(X=1) = P(S_1 \bar{S}_2 \bar{S}_3) + P(\bar{S}_1 S_2 \bar{S}_3) + P(\bar{S}_1 \bar{S}_2 S_3)$

$P(X=1) = P(S_1). \ P(\bar{S}_2/S_1). \ P[\bar{S}_3/(\bar{S}_2/S_1)] + P(\bar{S}_1). \ P(S_2/\bar{S}_1). \ P[\bar{S}_3/(S_2/\bar{S}_1)]$

$\qquad + P(\bar{S}_1). \ P(\bar{S}_2/\bar{S}_1). \ P[S_3/(\bar{S}_2/\bar{S}_1)]$

$\qquad = \dfrac{4}{10} \times \dfrac{6}{9} \times \dfrac{5}{8} + \dfrac{6}{10} \times \dfrac{4}{9} \times \dfrac{5}{8} + \dfrac{6}{10} \times \dfrac{5}{9} \times \dfrac{4}{8}$

$P(X=1) = \dfrac{1}{2}$

$P(X=2) = P(\bar{S}_1 S_2 S_3) + P(S_1 \bar{S}_2 S_3) + P(S_1 S_2 \bar{S}_3) = \dfrac{3}{10}$

$P(X=3) = P(S_1 S_2 S_3) = P(S_1). \ P(S_2/S_1). \ P[S_3/(S_2/S_1)] = \dfrac{1}{30}$

Ans.

X	0	1	2	3
P(X)	1/6	1/2	3/10	1/30

Check $\sum\limits_{x=0}^{3} p(x) = \dfrac{1}{6} + \dfrac{1}{2} + \dfrac{3}{10} + \dfrac{1}{30}$

$= \dfrac{5+15+9+1}{30} = \dfrac{30}{30} = 1$

15) Suppose the probability that 'an item produced by a particular machine is defective' is 0.2. If 10 items produced by this machine are selected at random, what is the probability that not more than one defective item is found? Use the binomial and Poisson distribution and compare the answers.

Solution

Probability 'p' that a product is defective is 0.2 i.e. p = 0.2

∴ q = 1- 0.2 = 0.8. n = 10. Let 'A' be the event 'Not more than 1 item is defective.'

∴ $P(A) = P(X = 0) + P(X = 1)$

Binomial distribution

$$^nC_r\, p^r\, q^{n-r} = P(X = r)$$

$$\therefore P(A) = {}^{10}C_0 (0.2)^0 \times (0.8)^{10} + {}^{10}C_1 (0.2)^1 \times (0.8)^9$$

$$= 1 \times 1 \times (\frac{8}{10})^{10} + 10 \times 0.2 \times (\frac{8}{10})^9$$

$$= (\frac{8}{10})^9 (\frac{8}{10} + 2) = \frac{14}{5} \times (\frac{8}{10})^9 = 0.3702$$

Poisson distribution

$$m = np = 10 \times 0.2 = 2$$

$$e^{-2} = 0.1353. \quad P(X = r) = \frac{m^r \times e^{-m}}{r!}$$

$$P(A) = P(0) + P(1)$$

$$= \frac{1 \times e^{-2}}{0!} + \frac{2 \times e^{-2}}{1}$$

$$= 3 \times e^{-2} = 3 \times 0.1353 = 0.4059$$

Two answers are 0.3702 and 0.4059 ≅ 0.4

16) A manufacturer of screws knows that 4% of his product is defective. If he sells the screws in boxes of 100, and guarantees that not more than five screws will be defective, what is the approximate probability that a box will fail to meet the guaranteed quality?

Solution:

Given p = 0.04, n = 100

m = np = 4, q = 1- 0.04 = 0.96

Event A – 'Not more than 5 screws will be defective'.

Assuming Poisson distribution,

$$P(X = r) \;=\; \frac{e^{-4} \times m^r}{r!}$$

$$P(A) \;=\; P(0) + P(1) + P(2) + P(3) + P(4) + P(5)$$

$$= \sum_{r=0}^{5} \frac{e^{-4} 4^r}{r!} = e^{-4}[1 + \frac{4}{1} + \frac{4^2}{2} + \frac{4^3}{6} + \frac{4^4}{24} + \frac{4^5}{120}] = 0.783$$

Event B – 'A box will fail to meet the guaranteed quality' i.e. A box has more than 5 defective screws.'

$$P(B) = 1 - P(A) = 1 - 0.783 = 0.217.$$

The answer is : The probability that a box will fail to meet the guaranteed quality is o.217. It is approximately 22%.

17) A bag 'A' contains 2 white and 3 red balls and Bag 'B' contains 4 white and 5 red balls. One ball is drawn at random from one of the bags and is found to be red. What is the probability that it was drawn from bag B?

Solution

   This is a problem on Inverse probability.

Event A – Bag A is chosen. P (A) $= \dfrac{1}{2}$

Event A – Bag B is chosen. P (A) $= \dfrac{1}{2}$

Let Event 'C' be 'ball drawn is red'

The probability of drawing

red ball under the condition that bag A is chosen is P (C/A) $= \dfrac{3}{5}$.

Similarly P (C/B) $= \dfrac{5}{9}$.

It is the probability of drawing a red ball under the condition that bag B is chosen. To determine P (B/C) i.e. the probability that the red ball drawn belonged to bag B;

$$P(B/C) = \frac{P(B).\ P(C/B)}{P(B).\ P(C/B) + P(A).\ P(C/A)}$$

$$P(B/C) = \frac{1/2 \times 5/9}{1/2 \times 5/9 + 1/2 \times 3/5} = \frac{5/9}{5/9 + 3/5}$$

$$= \frac{5 \times 45}{9 \times (25+27)}$$

Ans. $P(B/C) = \dfrac{25}{52}$

18) In a test, an examinee either guesses or copies or knows the answer to a multiple-choice question with four choices. The probability that he makes a guess is 1/3, he copies the answer is 1/6. The probability that his answer is correct, given that he copied it is 1/8. Find the probability that he knew the answer to the question, given that he correctly answered it.

<u>Solution:</u>

The three events are

(1) Event A – 'He guesses the answer'

(2) Event B – 'He copies it'

(3) Event C – 'He knows the answer'

An event E - 'Answer is correct'

$P(A) = \dfrac{1}{3}$, $P(B) = \dfrac{1}{6}$

$P(C) = 1 - P(A) - P(B)$ ∴ $P(C) = 1 - \dfrac{1}{3} - \dfrac{1}{6} = \dfrac{3}{6} = \dfrac{1}{2}$

The answer is correct given that he copies it, i.e. P(E/B) = 1/8.

The answer is correct given that he knows it i.e. P(E/C) = 1

The answer is correct given that he guesses it i.e. P(E/A) = 1/4 , he guesses one out of four choices.

Now, to determine P(C/E), i.e. the probability that he knows the answer given that the answer is correct,

$$P(C/E) = \frac{P(C).\ P(E/C)}{P(C).P(E/C) + P(B).\ P(E/B) + P(A).\ P(E/A)}$$

$$= \frac{1/2 \times 1}{1/2 \times 1 + 1/6 \times 1/8 + 1/3 \times 1/4}$$

$$= \frac{1/2}{1/2 + 1/48 + 1/12}$$

$$= \frac{24}{29}$$

Hence, the answer is $\frac{24}{29}$.

19) Six dice are thrown 729 times. How many times do you expect at least 3 dice to show 5 or 6?

X = No. of dice showing 5 or 6.

p = Probability of the event 'Getting 5 or 6 on a die'

$$p = \frac{2}{6} = \frac{1}{3}, q = 1 - \frac{1}{3} = \frac{2}{3}.$$

This is binomial distribution with n = 6.

$$P(X \geq 3) = 1 - [P(0) + P(1) + P(2)]$$

$$= 1 - [^6C_0 \, (\tfrac{1}{3})^0 \times (\tfrac{2}{3})^6 + {}^6C_1 \, (\tfrac{1}{3})^1 \times (\tfrac{2}{3})^5 + {}^6C_2 \, (\tfrac{1}{3})^2 \times (\tfrac{2}{3})^4]$$

$$= 1 - [(\tfrac{1}{3})^6 (2^6 + 6 \times 2^5 + 15 \times 2^4)]$$

Since, 3**6 = 729.

$$P(X \geq 3) = \frac{729 - (64 + 192 + 240)}{729} = \frac{233}{729}$$

It is expected that the event 'at least 3 dice show 5 or 6' occurs N times,

where N = (233/729) X 729 = 233.

∴ The Ans. is 233.

20) A man is known to speak truth 3 out of 4 times. He throws a die and reports that it is six. Find the probability that it is actually six.

Solution

    Event A - 'A man throws a die and reports six'

It is actually six i.e. 'A man tells the truth' – Event B_1

'The man does not tell truth.' - Event B_2

To find P(B1/A); the probability that it is actually six (man tells true) given that he reports six:

$P(B_1)$ = P (Man tells the truth) = 3/4

$P(B2)$ = P (Man tells lie) = 1 - 3/4 = 1/4

$P(A/B_1)$ = 1/6. Man reports 6 provided he tells truth. This is possible only when the outcome of throwing a die is 6, out of 6 possible outcomes.

Now, $P(A/B_2)$ = 5/6. Man reports 6 provided he tells lie. This is possible when the outcomes are other than 6. i.e. in 5 cases.

$$P(B_1/A) = \frac{P(B_1).\ P(A/B_1)}{P(B_1).\ P(A/B_1) + P(B_2).\ P(A/B_2)}$$

$$= \frac{\frac{3}{4} x \frac{1}{6}}{\frac{1}{6} x \frac{3}{4} + \frac{5}{6} x \frac{1}{4}} = \frac{\frac{3}{24}}{\frac{8}{24}}$$

$\therefore$ Ans.: $P(B_1/A) = \frac{3}{8}$.

21) By examining the chest X-ray, the probability that TB is detected when a person is actually suffering is 0.99. The probability that the doctor diagnoses incorrectly that a person has TB based on X-ray is 0.001. In a certain city, one in 1000 persons suffers from TB. A person is selected at random and is diagnosed to have TB. What is the chance that he actually has TB?

Solution:

A person is diagnosed to have TB – Event A

The person actually has TB - Event B_1

The person does not have TB - Event B_2

To find $P(B_1/A)$,

$P(B_1)$ = A person has TB = 1/1000 = 0.001

$P(B_2)$ = A person does not have TB = 1 – 0.001 = 0.999

$P(A/B_1)$ = X-ray diagnoses or detects TB when the person actually has TB = 0.99

$P(A/B_2)$ = The probability that a person is diagnosed to have TB when the person does not have TB = 0.001

Using the formula,

$$P(B_1/A) = \frac{P(B_1).\ P(A/B_1)}{P(B_1).\ P(A/B_1) + P(B_2).\ P(A/B_2)}$$

$$= \frac{0.001 \times 0.99}{0.001 \times 0.99 + 0.999 \times 0.001}$$

$$= \frac{0.99}{0.99 + 0.999} = \frac{0.99}{1.989} = \frac{110}{221}$$

Hence, the answer is $\frac{110}{221}$

Chapter 8

APPLICATIONS OF PROBABILITY THEORY

1)   Evolution of Probability theory

This section is based on the study of one of the interesting outcomes of 'Google search on 'Probability Theory, Applications', titled 'Beginnings of Modern Probability Theory'

Probability emerged in the seventeenth century as a systematic mathematical study. Its history in 18th and 19th centuries provides a fascinating study of the shifting attitudes and hopes of the enlightenment for clarity and certainty. The mathematical probablists tended to be ambitious about extending their analytical methodology into many different fields.

One of the first publications of mathematical probability is by Dutch mathematicians Huygens and DeWitt. It contained the study of mathematical expectations, a series of analysis of the different expectations in various games of dice. DeWitt also extended the mathematics of probability to analyze annuities on the basis of mortality.

In eighteenth century Jakob Bernoulli interpreted probability as a state of mind. At that time the standard belief was 'There was no randomness in the world. All things which exist or acted upon under the sun; past, present, future things, always have the greatest certainty. As a mental state the probability is the degree of certainty .This definition marked a shift away from expectations to probability, and from equi-probable outcomes to measures of certainty. Bernoulli's theorem states that the probability that observed frequencies come closer to a priori mathematical calculations of probabilities, increases with number of trials. For example, consider an experiment of throwing a fair die. Mathematics says that the probability of any one of six outcomes is one is to six. As the number of throws (n) increases, number of times any one number (say, 5) shows, goes closer to the value (n/6).

In the late 17th century, the development of natural theology and empirical science fostered the idea of uncertainty of all human knowledge. The proof a hypothesis need not have the full vigor of a mathematical proof. What mattered was a particular level of certainty such that a reasonable person would accept it. Thus, the faith became a matter of sufficient evidence for acceptance.

In France, in 18th century, one urgent issue prompted much argument about probability. The conservative opinion was strongly against inoculation against smallpox. Daniel Bernoulli applied his formulae for lotteries to the problem. His results favored inoculation. D'Alembert, analyzing Bernoulli's formulae questioned whether individual social behavior could ever match mathematical analysis of it. For him, the calculus of probability was primarily descriptive of common psychology of risk and not prescriptive. Making too much reliance on mathematics led to problems, particularly when mathematical results did not fit good sense. Finally, the attempt to base the concept of 'reasonable individual' on the mathematical probabilities of expectations failed as the reasonable individual turned out to be too complex and elusive a concept to fit mathematical measurements.

Life Insurance offered an excellent example, in early 19th century, to defend the utility of probability theory. The regularities among large samples over longer periods of time confirmed a strict determinism. Society for Equitable Assurance on Lives and survivorship attempted to apply mathematical probability to life insurance premiums. Their principles in establishing premiums were grounded on the expectancy of the continuance of life. The lives of men separately taken are uncertain, yet in aggregate of lives, it is reducible to a certainty.

The success of this new form of statistical thinking had effects far beyond life insurance. One need not take into account individual behavior, what mattered was the information revealed in the study of very large groups over a long time. Thus, the attention was shifted from the concept of 'reasonable person', as the criterion to the statistically quantifiable behavior of the entire group. Thus, in mid- 19th century, the interest of probabilists shifted from questions of individual judgment to problems of computed averages in large population.

In the study of population statistics, called social physics, Adolphe Quetelet derived the concept of 'average man'. The 'average man' of Quetelet was a fiction. Nevertheless, it was made a criterion by which society should be analyzed. His law of errors analyzed the departures from the average, but did not lead to any study of systematic distribution of error.

In 1888, December there was a transition from classical theory to modern theory. It signaled a turn away from averages towards the systematic study of differences or departures from average.Quetelet and Laplace, coming from the astronomical tradition, sought uniformity. They interpreted deviations from average as the result of error. They were to get rid of or to provide a just allowance for it. On the other hand, Galton had primary interest in biology and was concerned with variety and individual differences. These deviations were the thing he wanted to preserve and know about. Gauss developed the concept of law of errors to deal with the difficulty that all astronomical observations and measurements are subject to some random error. Gaussian law and several other distributions find applications in different fields.

In conclusion, the probability theory has gone through many changes; from probability of expectation to that of a successful outcome, to the concept of a reasonable person, to average value, to distribution of departures from average value.

2) Application Fundamentals

The application procedure, in general, involves four steps. The first step is a collection of data. It should be carried out systematically with a definite aim in view. Data should be collected for each and every unit of whole lot, called population. It should be conducted with much accuracy .There are two types of data, digital and continuous; and there are three types of population based on its size; small, large or very large. Some times, complete enumeration is prohibitively expensive and time consuming. Therefore, in case of large population a sample consisting of a few of them is selected systematically. This sample is then treated as population for next step.

The second step is representation of data. The collected data, called raw data, is divided into a convenient number of groups, called classes. The width of a class is called 'class interval' and its mid value is called class-mark. The number of items falling in a class is called its frequency. A table is prepared, showing class interval, class mark and corresponding class frequency. This table is called frequency or frequency distribution table. This data may be represented graphically.

The third step, analysis, involves mathematical calculations; various examples are covered in previous chapters. The fourth step is called 'statistical inference '. It involves conclusions and intelligent comments, regarding decisions, predictions or prescriptions. These steps, particularly the last two steps, require additional knowledge, basic and advanced level, of the particular field of application. Some fields of application are quantum mechanics, kinetic theory, astronomy, moral science, management, and the list is endless.

3) Sampling

A sample is a small section selected from a population to represent it. Sampling is a process of drawing a sample. Sampling aims at gathering maximum information of the population with minimum effort, cost and time. The logic of sampling theory is the logic of induction, in which we pass from particular (sample) to general (population). From the results of analysis of a sample we draw conclusions about the population. In random sampling each member of population has equal chance of selection. Random selection of a member can be done in many ways, by using a table of random numbers or by a computer generated sequence of random numbers or by picking up a chit from a hat or a box, or by a mechanical device like a turning wheel used in games of luck. A stratified random sampling is used when a population is not homogeneous. The population is then divided into homogeneous subgroups of perhaps unequal size. A sample is then drawn from each homogeneous subgroup to represent it. The number of samples from a subgroup may or may not be proportional to its size. This method gives greater statistical precision or smaller value of variance, since the variability within a subgroup is lower than that of the whole population.

A complex method, called multistage sampling is used in applied social research. For example, consider a survey of school students on national level. .First sub-grouping is based on geography, as per states. From each state, a sample of districts is selected randomly. A sample of schools is chosen randomly from each selected district. From each selected school a sample of students is selected randomly. And, finally, the required information is collected from each selected student to complete the first step of data collection.

There is no hard and fast rule that decides the number of sub groups or the number of samples representing a group. These factors are decided by the judgments of an experienced organizer.

4)   Analysis of Sampled Data

In case of small population, the data is digital and 'n 'the number of samples is small. It is represented by a table or by a histogram. The required statistical parameters are then calculated. In chapter 7, we have considered many numerical examples illustrating analysis of small data to calculate different probabilities. There are several other parameters, other than probability like mean, mode, median values. In case of large population, the sample size, n, is equal to or greater than thirty; it is not too large to be handled as a single group. The ratio (n/N), sample size to population size, is decided not by any mathematical rule hence it changes from population to population. It may take any value from about five to twenty percent, depending upon the variability of the population. Now, a frequency or probability distribution curve is drawn for a chosen group of samples. In many cases it is a normal or Gaussian curve. We have already covered the mathematical details of this distribution. In the literature one comes across a large number (about 50) of distributions. Some are continuous (about 30) and some are discrete. Some of the well known distributions are: Poisson, Normal, Rectangular, and Exponential. In quantum mechanic, Fermi-Dirac probability function, Bose-Einstein distribution function, and Maxwell-Boltzmann distribution are used.

When the size of population is very large; a single sample group drawn to represent the population is so large that it is difficult to represent it for analysis purpose. So, a number of sample groups each of reasonable size are drawn. Then, each sample group is separately analyzed. And a set consisting of a required parameter of each group is treated as a new" collected data "and this data is further analyzed.

5)   Statistical Inference

This is the last but not the least step of the application procedure. The required parameters are calculated using the results of the analysis. These are the parameters of the group. Finally, the required parameter of single individual is estimated and final conclusion is arrived at. It will be interesting to consider some examples of chapter 7. In each case we shall draw a statistical inference.

In examples of the chapter 7, simple applications of the probability theory are covered. It is interesting to refer to some of them to carry out the last step of the application procedure. A statistical inference can be based on the calculation results obtained. Referring to example 3, the answer is P (A) = 4/7, P (B) =2/7 and P(C) =1/7. Among the three people A is most likely to win, however his chance of winning is not very good as his probability of winning is less than sixty percent. The answer of example 4 is that the probability of a student passing in both the papers is 3/20 i.e. 15 %. The conclusion is that the examination is difficult to pass. A student is advised to treat the examination more seriously. The answer of example 5 is that the probability of throwing 17 is 1/72 i.e. about 1.5 %. So, the conclusion is that the sum 17 is not a good bet. Some more analysis is required to recommend a good bet. In example 8, the answer is that the probability of exactly two children are chosen on the committee is 3/7, that is about 43 %. Since the probability is small, it cannot be predicted that the committee of four will have exactly two children. Some more data and analysis is required for good prediction. In case of example 9, the answer that the probability of the outcome 'all the three balls are different' is 40/143, that is less than 30 %. The second answer is that the probability of the outcome 'all of same colour 'is 9/143, that is less than 7 %. Both the probabilities are small. It is necessary to carry out more analysis to predict the most likely outcome. The answer of the example 10 is that the probability of the outcome 'both are white' is 1/7, that is 14 %. Thus it is not a good bet. Consider the example 14. The answer is a table, giving the probability distribution of the number of white balls drawn. The highest value is P (X=1) = 1/2, that is 50 %. The most probable outcome is that, one white ball is drawn when three balls are drawn one by one without replacement, from a bag containing 4 white and 6 red balls. Nevertheless, it is not recommended to have high stakes, as the probability of winning is 50 % only. The answer of the example 16 is that the event, 'a box will fail to meet the guaranteed quality i.e. a box has more than 5 defective screws', has a probability of about 22 %. The conclusion is that 22% of the customers each buying a box of 100 screws is likely to complain and the manufacturer may have to replace about 22 boxes out of 100 boxes. So, it is better to improve the quality of screw making or avoid giving a guarantee that 'not more than 5 screws will be defective.' The example 18 is interesting. Based on the calculations and the given data, one may conclude that a student who gives correct answer really knows the answer. This is true because, the calculations result is that the probability that he knows the answer given that his answer is correct is 24/29 i.e. about 80 %. The answer of the example 21 is that the probability that a person really has TB, given that the person is diagnosed to have TB is equal to 110/221 i.e. about 50 %. The conclusion is; the probability of a person to have TB is increased from 0.001 to 0.5 as he is diagnosed to have TB. He need not panic but he must undergo more tests to confirm the diagnosis, before going to take the treatment.

6)   Testing of Hypothesis

Let us consider one example. A die is thrown 9000 times. Throw of 5 or 6 is obtained 3240 times. On the assumption of random throwing, do the data indicate an unbiased die?

The probability of throwing 5 or 6 is P (5) +P (6) = 1/3. It is assumed here that the die is unbiased, so each of the 6 outcomes is equally probable. Theoretical frequency of the event 5 or 6 is equal to 9000. (1/3) =3000. So the deviation is 3240 -3000 = 240.Assuming binomial distribution, the value of standard deviation,(= (npq)**0.5), is 44.72. Now, the value of the normalized variate (z) is (240 / 44.72 = 5.4). Since the number of observation is large, binomial distribution approaches normal curve. Using the properties of normal curve, z<=2.58 for 1% level of significance. Since the value of z is 5.4, that is much greater than 2.58, it is concluded that the assumption or hypothesis is not correct. The die is biased.

7)   Application to advising on a genetic test.

In case of a rare genetic disease, the statistics says that only one in a million people carry it. A genetic test is extremely good. A statistics says that it is 100% sensitive, i.e. it is always correct if you have the disease. And it is 99.99 % specific, i.e. it gives a false positive result only 0.01 % of the time. Usually people are reluctant to go in for such a test. Bayes theorem can be applied to calculate, and the results of calculations will help to guide individuals.

When a person takes the test there are four possible situations. (1) Person is healthy and the test is positive. (2) Person is sick and the test is positive. (3) Person is healthy and the test is negative. (4) Person is sick and the test is negative. Let the event X be "person is healthy." Let the event Y be "the test is positive." The data collected is: The test is 100 percent correct if one has the disease. .That is P(Y/not X) =1 and P (not Y/ not X) =0. Secondly, it is 99.99% specific i.e. P (not Y/X) = 0.9999 and P(Y/ X) = 0.0001. Thirdly, statistics says that only one in a million people carry it; i.e. P (not X) = 1/1000000 = 0.000001, and P(X) = 0.999999.

Consider the first situation. P(X/Y), the probability that person is healthy given that the test is positive, is given by P(Y/X).P(X)/ P(Y); where P(Y) = P(Y/not X). P (not X) + P(Y/X).P(X).On substituting the values we get the probability is equal to 99.01%. Similarly remaining probabilities are calculated. P (not X/ Y) =1% (approx.), P (X/not Y) = 100%. And P (not X/not Y) = 0 %. It shows that if the test is negative, a person does not have the rare genetic disease. If the test result is positive, it is likely that the person is suffering from the rare genetic disease. Before the test, the possibility of a person having the disease is one in a million; where as on testing positive the possibility of the person having the disease increases to 1 % i.e. one in hundred.

The advice is a person should undergo the test. If tested negative one can relax as the result shows 100 % healthy. If tested positive, the probability of having the disease is increased to one in hundred i.e. increased 10000 times. One need not panic but should go in for one more test.

8)   Gambling

Gambling is a game of chance. The probability theory plays a big role in predictions of the results in gambling. We have already considered several experiments of 'throwing of a die', 'tossing coins,' and 'drawing a card from a pack of cards'. These are simplest forms of games of chance and introduce to what mathematics in games of chance means.

The technical processes of a game stand for experiments that generate aleatory events. The events can be identified with sets, namely, the parts of the sample space. The complete mathematical model is given by the probability field attached to the experiment. It consists of three parts; sample space, field of events, and probability function. Any predictable event in gambling, no matter how complex, can be decomposed into elementary events with respect to the union of sets. All the properties of probability can be applied in the practical calculus in gambling to find the numerical probability of the event of interest.

In 6/49 lottery, the experiment of drawing six numbers from the 49 generates events such as, drawing six specific numbers, drawing five numbers from the six specific numbers, drawing four from the six specific numbers, drawing at least one number from a certain group of numbers etc. The sample space of the experiment is the set of all 6-size combinations of numbers from the 49.

9)   Theory of errors

A measurement process is characterized by three types of errors; accidental errors, systematic errors and random errors. When a measurement is repeated several times under identical conditions, the results may not be identical. Almost all the results are close to each other. Only those results which largely deviate from others are considered as erratic, caused by accidental errors. These are therefore discarded. It is a practice to find the arithmetic mean of the results and accept it as the true value of the measurand. This mean value is the correct value if no systematic error is present. The averaging process eliminates random error. Secondly, one is interested in another characteristic of measurement process. It is called 'Precision index'. It is a measure of consistency or repeatability of a single measurement. Different terms used to express the precision are; variance, standard deviation, and probable error.

Variance = Mean square deviation.

Standard deviation = Root mean square deviation.

Probable Error = 0.6745 x standard deviation.

Mostly the probability distribution of random error is a normal curve. The probability that a single measurement result has a random part of error less than the standard deviation is sixty eight percent. Also the probability that, in a single measurement the error is less than the probable error is fifty percent.

BIBLIOGRAPHY

1) Dr. Grewal, B.S. (1993). *Higher Engineering Mathematics* (29th edition) (Ch.22). Delhi: Khanna Publishers.

2) Dr. Joseph Mathew, & Anandvally, K.L. (2004). *Systematic Approach to Mathematics Part A (Ch.9).* Trivandrum: Chand Publications.

3) Dr. Joseph Mathew, & Anandvally, K.L. (2004). *Systematic Approach to Mathematics Part C* (Ch.6) Trivandrum: Chand Publications.

4) Prof. Janardhanan Pillay, C.P. (1989). *Second- year Pre-degree Mathematics.* Ottapalam, Kerala: Ajith Book Centre

5) Harris, Forest K.(1968). *Electrical Measurements. (Ch.1)* New Delhi: Wiley Eastern Private Ltd.

6) NCERT. (2005). Mathematics, (textbook for class 11). (Chs. 1,2,7 and 16)

7) NCERT. (2006). *Mathematics. Part 2, (textbook for class 12).* (Ch.13)

8) Zhaxybayeva, Olga. (1998). *Example of using Bayes' Theorem.* Retrieved January 27, 2009, from Olga Zhaxybayeva Home Page Web site: http://carrot.mcb.uconn.edu/~olgazh/bayes_th_problem.html

9) Johnston, Ian C. (1999). *The Beginnings of Modern Probability Theory.* (Section Four, A Handbook for the Early History of Modern Science). Retrieved February 2, 2009, from johnstonia Home Page Web site: http://records.viu.ca/~johnstoi/darwin/title.html

10) Trochim, William M.K. (2006). *Probability Sampling.* Retrieved January 27, 2009, from Research Methods Knowledge Base Web site: http://www.Socialresearchmethods.net/kb/sampprob.php

11) Infarom Publishing. *Gambling.* Retrieved March 5, 2009, from Probability Theory Guide and Applications. Home page Website: http://probability. infarom. ro/gambling.html

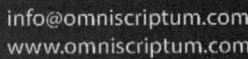

Printed by Books on Demand GmbH, Norderstedt / Germany